US AGAINST WHATEVER

A KARAOKE CABARET

Written by Maureen Lennon
In collaboration with Nastazja Somers
Music by James Frewer
Lyrics by Paul Smith

Cast

Anna / 3 – Edyta Budnik
Steph / 2 – Josie Morley
MC / Sheila / Dean Windass / Nigel Farage – Emma Thornett
Tara / 1 / Interviewer – Sèverine Howell-Meri
Neil / 4 / Man / Jordan – Joshua Meredith
Michal / The Doctor / 5 – Adam Hadi

Creative Team

Writer – Maureen Lennon
Collaborator – Nastazja Somers
Director – Paul Smith
Composer and Musical Director – James Frewer
Designer – Bethany Wells
Lighting Designer – Jess Addinall
Sound Designer – Ed Clarke
Projection Designer – Daniel Denton
Movement Director – Adam Hadi
Assistant Director and Dramaturg – Matthew May
Drum Supervisor – Joshua Meredith
Script Support – Meg Badorek-Miszczuk

Production Team

Production Manager – Emily Anderton
DSM – Danielle Harris
Stage Manager, Hull – Shona Wright
Stage Manager, Liverpool – Helen Lainsbury

In association with Liverpool Everyman & Playhouse
and Hull Truck Theatre

Developed with the support of the National Theatre,
British Council and Polish Cultural Institute

Maureen Lennon (Writer)

Theatre includes: *Gobble, The Washerwomen's Warning* (Bellow);
Bare Skin On Briny Waters (Bellow, with Tabitha Mortiboy);
The Cautionary Tale of Horrid Ham Carver (Bellow, with Tabitha
Mortiboy); *The Way Home* (Paines Plough: Come To Where I'm
From); *A Long Morning Quiet* (Sheffield Theatres: 4x15).

Maureen is an associate artist of Middle Child and a Leeds
Playhouse FUSE writer. In 2017 she was shortlisted for the
Walter Swan Prize and *Bare Skin On Briny Waters* received two
award commendations from the NSDF Edinburgh Award.

Nastazja Somers (Collaborator)

As theatre director: *10* (VAULT Festival).

Originally from Poland Nastazja is a London-based theatremaker
and activist. She is the founder of HerStory: Intersectional
feminist festival and co-founder of DANGEROUS SPACE, an all
female company. Nastazja has made work both in the UK as well
as internationally. She is currently finalising her Masters in Applied
Theatre at the Royal Central School of Speech and Drama.

Paul Smith (Director)

Paul is a founding member and the artistic director of Middle Child.

For Middle Child: *One Life Stand* (Paines Plough Roundabout/
UK Tour); *All We Ever Wanted Was Everything* (Bush Theatre/
Paines Plough Roundabout); *I Hate Alone*; *Ten Storey Love
Song*; *Weekend Rockstars*; *Mercury Fur* and *Saturday Night &
Sunday Morning*.

Paul is an associate artist of Hull Truck Theatre, where he was
assistant director on *The Rise and Fall of Little Voice* and *A Taste of
Honey*. He graduated from the LAMDA Directing Course in 2011.

James Frewer (Composer and Musical Director)

For Middle Child: *One Life Stand* (Paines Plough Roundabout/
UK Tour); *I Hate Alone*; *All We Ever Wanted Was Everything*
(Bush Theatre/Paines Plough Roundabout); *Mercury Fur*;
Weekend Rockstars; *Modern Life Is Rubbish* and *Saturday Night
& Sunday Morning.*

Theatre includes:

As composer: *Mixtape* (Royal Exchange); *The Hundred and One Dalmatians* (Birmingham Rep); *Twelfth Night* (Orange Tree); *Folk* (Birmingham Rep/Watford Palace/Hull Truck Theatre); *Get Carter* (Northern Stage/UK Tour); *Sleeping Beauty*; *Cinderella*; *A Taste of Honey* (Hull Truck Theatre); *The Thing About Psychopaths* (Red Ladder Theatre/UK Tour).

As musical director and performer: *The Snow Queen* (New Vic Theatre); *Dancehall* (Cast Doncaster); *The Night Before Christmas* (Soho Theatre); *This House* (National Theatre, dep performer).

As sound designer: *The Season Ticket* (Pilot Theatre/Northern Stage); *This Land*; *Red Sky at Night* (Pentabus); *A Further Education*; *Deluge* (Hampstead Theatre); *Love Me Do* (Watford Palace Theatre); *The Ugly Sisters* (Rash Dash/UK Tour).

James is an associate artist of Middle Child.

Bethany Wells (Designer)

For Middle Child: *All We Ever Wanted Was Everything* (Bush Theatre/Paines Plough Roundabout).

Recent work includes: *Legacy* (York Theatre Royal); *TRUST* (Gate Theatre); *Party Skills for the End of the World* (Nigel Barrett/ Louise Mari); *The Department of Distractions*; *The Desire Paths*; *Partus* (Third Angel); *Cosmic Scallies* (Graeae/Royal Exchange); *We Were Told There Was Dancing*; *The Factory* (Royal Exchange Young Company); *Removal Men* (Yard Theatre); *Dark Corners* (Polar Bear); *Seen and Not Heard* (Complicite Creative Learning); *THE FUTURE* (Company 3); *Late Night Love* (Eggs Collective); *Live Art Dining* (Live Art Bistro); *Race Cards* (Selina Thompson); *Correspondence* (Old Red Lion Theatre); *My Eyes Went Dark* (Finborough Theatre); *WINK* (Theatre 503).

Bethany is an associate artist of Middle Child.

Jess Addinall (Lighting Designer)

Theatre includes: *Ugly Duckling* (The Herd); *The Ballad of Paragon Station* (Hester Ullyart); *Beach Body Ready* (The Roaring Girls); *Macbeth* (RSC Schools); *60 Seconds* (in association with The Roaring Girls) and *The Children* (Hull Truck Youth Theatre).

Jess is the associate lighting designer for The Roaring Girls and is a technician at Hull Truck Theatre.

Ed Clarke (Sound Designer)

For Middle Child: *All We Ever Wanted Was Everything* (Bush Theatre/Paines Plough Roundabout); *One Life Stand* (Paines Plough Roundabout/UK Tour).

Theatre includes: *Leave Taking*; *The Royale*; *The Invisible*; *Perseverance Drive*; *Fear* (Bush Theatre); *A Super Happy Story (About Feeling Super Sad)* (Silent Uproar); *A Christmas Carol*; *A Short History of Tractors in Ukrainian* (Hull Truck Theatre); *Showboat* (New London Theatre); *The Infidel* (Theatre Royal Stratford East); *Orpheus* (Little Bulb Theatre at BAC/worldwide); *Baddies* (Unicorn Theatre); *The Realness*; *Politrix*; *Phoenix*; *KnifeEdge* and *Babylon* (The Big House); *Beauty and the Beast* (Young Vic/worldwide); *Danny Boyle's Frankenstein* (National Theatre); *Backbeat* (Duke of York's Theatre); *The Mysteries* and *The Good Hope* (National Theatre); *The Railway Children* (Waterloo International Station/Roundhouse Theatre Toronto); *Fatal Attraction* (Theatre Royal Haymarket); *His Teeth* (Only Connect Theatre); *Baby Doll* (Albery Theatre); *Alex* (Arts Theatre/UK and International tour) and *Old Times, A Doll's House* (Donmar Warehouse).

Ed was nominated for the Olivier Award for *Danny Boyle's Frankenstein* in 2012. He is an associate artist of Middle Child.

Daniel Denton (Projection Designer)

Design credits include: *The Little Prince* (Protein Dance); *Sundowing* (Kali Theatre Company); *James Graham's: Sketching* (Wilston's Music Hall); *On Raftery's Hill* (Abbey Theatre); *Misty* (Bush Theatre/Trafalgar Studios); *As You Like It* (Theatre by the Lake); *Flashdance: The Musical* (UK/International Tour); *To Love Somebody Melancholy* (UK Tour); *Ready Or Not* (Arcola Theatre/UK Tour); *Peter Pan* (Exeter Northcott Theatre); *Bumblescratch* (Adelphi Theatre); *Biedermann and the Arsonists* (Sadler's Wells).

Daniel is an associate of video design collective Mesmer.

Adam Hadi (Cast and Movement Director)

Adam has five years of acting experience with Pijana Sypialnia Theatre, Warsaw and is soon to graduate from the Faculty of Acting of the Warsaw Film School.

Matthew May (Assistant Director and Dramaturg)

For Middle Child as an actor:

As an actor: *Ten Storey Love Song*; *Saturday Night & Sunday Morning* and *Modern Life Is Rubbish.*

Theatre includes: *Pig* (Silent Uproar).

Matthew is a founding member of Middle Child.

Joshua Meredith (Cast and Drum Supervisor)

For Middle Child: *All We Ever Wanted Was Everything* (Bush Theatre/Paines Plough Roundabout); *Cinderella.*

Theatre includes: *After Miss Julie* (Bleviss Laboratory Theatre); *Much Ado About Nothing* (The Lord Chamberlain's Men); *Services No Longer Required* (BBC Philharmonic Orchestra); *Sam Wanamaker Festival* (Globe Theatre); *Cock* (Joue Le Genre); Departure Lounge (InStep Theatre); *The Night Season*; *Austen* and *Great Expectations* (East Riding Theatre); *Jack and the Beanstalk*; *Cinderella* (Stafford Gatehouse Theatre); *Loot* and *Funny Turns* (Hull Truck Theatre).

Edyta Budnik (Cast)

Theatre includes: *Albion* (Almeida); *Tense/Nine* (Nabokov); *Under the Lid* (Jermyn Theatre).

Television includes: *Killing Eve*; *Casualty*; *Doctors*; *The Sarah Jane Adventures* (BBC); *Coronation Street*; *The Bletchley Circle* (ITV); *The Tunnel* (Sky Atlantic); *The Bill* (Talkback Thames).

Film includes: *Leonor Short* (NFTS); *Breaking Free* (Jellyfish Films); *Chronophobe* (Rainstar Productions).

Josie Morley (Cast)

For Middle Child: *Weekend Rockstars*; *Modern Life Is Rubbish*; *Jack and the Beanstalk*; *Aladdin*; *Dick Whittington*; *Cinderella* and *Beauty and the Beast.*

Theatre includes: *It's Different For Girls* (She Productions); *The Kings Of Hull*; *Long Live The Kings Of Hull* (Hull New Theatre); *Beach Body Ready* (The Roaring Girls); *Broken Little Robots*; *Cosmic* (Hull Truck Theatre); *This Might Hurt* and *The Empty Nesters' Club* (John Godber Co./Wakefield Theatre Royal); *Omniscience* (Brick by Brick).

Sèverine Howell-Meri (Cast)

Theatre includes: *Cinderella and the Beanstalk* (Theatre 503).

Television includes: *Casualty*; *Doctors* (BBC); *Disconnect* (Channel 4).

Film includes: *Don't Stutter*.

Sèverine has also performed at the Lyric Hammersmith as part of the Young Harts Writers' Competition, and at the Bush Theatre in *Bottled*.

Emma Thornett (Cast)

Theatre includes: *The Producers* (Royal Exchange Theatre); *Exit the King (U/S)*; *Warhorse* (National Theatre); *101 Dalmatians* (Birmingham Rep); *Darkness Darkness* (Nottingham Playhouse); *The Browning Version (U/S)*; *South Downs (U/S)* (Harold Pinter Theatre).

Television includes: *Extras*; *Double Take* (BBC).

THEATRE THAT MAKES A NOISE

Middle Child are an award-winning Hull-based company creating gig theatre that brings people together for a good night out with big ideas. We tell untold stories which capture the electrifying moment when the beat drops, mixing original live music with bold new writing. Our events are live and loud, making sense of the modern world.

'Middle Child claim on their website: "We will set fire to your expectations of what a night at the theatre can be." Yeah, right. But they really do.' *Telegraph*

We are committed to breaking down barriers and ensuring that theatre is affordable and accessible for all. We will set fire to your expectations of what a night at the theatre can be. We are an associate company of Paines Plough and an Arts Council England National Portfolio Organisation, supported by Absolutely Cultured and Hull City Council.

'Here's to FUN/LOUD theatre for ppl who don't go because the last time they went was year9 Hamlet and they didn't get it.' @Steph_Martin_ on Twitter

Awards include:
All We Ever Wanted Was Everything
(Broadway Baby Bobby Award 2017)

All We Ever Wanted Was Everything
(The 730 Review Best of the Best 2017)

Ten Storey Love Song
(Broadway Baby Bobby Award 2016)

Weekend Rockstars
(Musical Theatre Network Development Award 2015)

Middle Child are

Artistic Director	Paul Smith
Executive Director	Lindsey Alvis
General Manager	Emily Anderton
Communications Manager	Jamie Potter
Company Members	Mungo Beaumont
	Ellen Brammar
	Emma Bright
	Sophie Clay
	Edward Cole
	Marc Graham
	Matthew May
	James Stanyer

Board of Directors
Martin Green CBE (Chair); Sharon Darley, Jane Fallowfield,
Meg Badorek-Miszczuk, Aysha Powell and David Watson.
Associate Artists
Luke Barnes, Alice Beaumont, Ed Clarke, James Frewer,
Maureen Lennon, Bethany Wells, Tom Wells and Natalie Young.

Middle Child is a company limited by guarantee.
Registered company number: 9921306

Middle Child

Darley's
Porter Street
Hull
HU1 2JE
+44 (0) 1482 221857
office@middlechildtheatre.co.uk
middlechildtheatre.co.uk

Follow @middlechildhull on Twitter and Instagram.
Like Middle Child at facebook.com/middlechildhull

  Supported using public funding by **ARTS COUNCIL ENGLAND**

LIVERPOOL
everyman
&PLAYHOUSE
theatres

Liverpool Everyman & Playhouse are two distinct theatres, which together make up a single artistic force.

We are driven by our passion for our art-form, our love of our city and our unswerving belief that theatre at its best can enhance lives. While our two performance bases could hardly be more different, they are united by our commitment to brilliant, humane, forward-thinking theatre that responds to its time and place.

Discovering and supporting new talent is at the heart of what we do, whether that's through the work of our New Works team who run regular development opportunities, playwright support and events for new writers and theatre makers or our award winning youth engagement programme, Young Everyman Playhouse (YEP); recognised by the Arts Council as a youth arts exemplar.

Since the re-opening of the Everyman in 2014 the theatres have received numerous awards including the prestigious RIBA Stirling Prize for Architecture and the UK Theatre Award for promoting diversity.

Supported by Liverpool City Council and the Arts Council England.

Artistic Director: Gemma Bodinetz
everymanplayhouse.com
0151 709 4776

Hull Truck Theatre is a pioneering theatre with a unique northern voice, locally rooted, global in outlook, inspiring artists, audiences and communities to reach their greatest potential.

We produce and present inspiring theatre that reflects the diversity of a modern Britain. We provide the resources, space and support to grow people and ideas, are an ambassador for our city, a flagship for our region and a welcoming home for our communities.

Through our work with schools and local communities we engage with thousands of young people, disabled groups and adults, offering opportunities to participate in the arts, whether as the first step into a career, a way to build confidence and meet new people, or as part of a rounded education.

We are continuing the momentum of Hull 2017 to tell inspiring stories dug from the heart of our city, alongside tales from the wider world, that reflect the diverse range of communities and creative voices that populate our nation. We are ambitious and bold, committed to our core values of Inclusion, Innovation and Integrity.

Hull Truck Theatre gratefully acknowledges support from Arts Council England and Hull City Council.

US AGAINST WHATEVER

US AGAINST WHATEVER

Written by Maureen Lennon
in collaboration with Nastazja Somers

Music by James Frewer
Lyrics by Paul Smith

OBERON BOOKS
LONDON

WWW.OBERONBOOKS.COM

First published in 2019 by Oberon Books Ltd
521 Caledonian Road, London N7 9RH
Tel: +44 (0) 20 7607 3637 / Fax: +44 (0) 20 7607 3629
e-mail: info@oberonbooks.com
www.oberonbooks.com

PB ISBN: 9781786827425
E ISBN: 9781786827432

Cover photography: Anna Bean

Printed and bound by 4EDGE Limited, Hockley, Essex, UK.
eBook conversion by Lapiz Digital Services, India.

Visit www.oberonbooks.com to read more about all our books and to buy them. You
will also find features, author interviews and news of any author events, and you can
sign up for e-newsletters so that you're always first to hear about our new releases.

Printed on FSC accredited paper

10 9 8 7 6 5 4 3 2 1

There is a drumroll.

The MC takes her position and is hit by a spotlight.

She is wearing a smart, serious suit.

Welcome To Our Very Serious Play About Brexit

Everyone's talking about it ('bout it)
Everyone's thinking about it
Gotta make some art about it ('bout it)
Gotta make a play about it

Yes it is the word on everybody's lips,
The buzzword on which the conversation flips,
A compound word of Britain and exit,
Which upon hearing everyone legs it
But you chose to buy yourself a ticket
To join us here and see if we can crack it
(Off mic, spoken.) Doubt it.

So everybody here tonight (hi)
Those of you in the good seats (how do you do)
Those of you on the front row (brave)
Those of you in the cheap seats (we appreciate it's a difficult
time of financial uncertainty and we're only just coming out
of austerity, we get it we do, it's really fine, expensive theatre
seats aren't exactly a priority at this difficult time)
It is our duty tonight to present to you
Present to you
Present to you

(Spoken.) Our very serious and worthy play about Brexit
Oh, we're gonna cause some disagreements
Probably about those trade agreements
Free market, the economy, Boris' bus
British autonomy
If you vote Labour we'll piss you off
If you vote Tory we'll piss you off

If you voted Leave or voted Remain,
You'll treat tonight with disdain
If you don't eat meat or you hate the poor,
If you read books or come from Ecuador
Whoever you are and whatever you do

This is probably not the play for you
Because there's one thing on which we're all agreed
Which the Queen herself has probably decreed
The world doesn't need
No, the country doesn't need
And this city certainly doesn't need

(Spoken.) Our very serious and worthy play about Brexit

Now you're through the door
It's time for
You've paid for
Our very serious and worthy play about Brexit.

The music continues underneath as we move into a silhouetted Posh English Tea Party.

It is SERIOUS and DULL and feels RIDICULOUS.

Interlude: Posh English Tea Party

All the characters play exaggerated versions of concern. They are not listening to each other even when they respond. Sometimes they nod and make noises at inappropriate or random moments.

1 Well I voted to Leave to reduce the undemocratic nature of the legislative process, and UK obligations to EU implemented directives.

MC Exactly. Do you want another cuppa?

2 Really I was torn because I do believe the EU's a neoliberalist organisation with an ultimately destructive agenda, but, the terms of the conversation did become skewed in a nationalist direction.

1 The poster.

2 Exactly Nigel Farage and the poster.

MC I see. Very interesting. Anything to feed in?

1 Well as we were discussing just over breakfast /

2 This morning /

3 Yes just this morning wasn't it. I really think we have to question whether Jeremy Corbyn should be held partially responsible for the result because he never truly committed to the Remain campaign /

5 Mmm it's a good point.

1 It is.

MC Exactly. Exactly. Thank you. Have an orange juice.

3 Thank you.

2 And then there's Boris Johnson /

MC Yes Boris/

2 And his bus/

MC Of course of course. Please let's discuss

Boris.

4 Of course. Let's. Can I have a muffin?

MC Feel free feel free. Coffee anyone?

5 And all those discussions we had about the two thousand-and-something directive about shipping /

3 Oh right yes. All those round the dinner table.

2 That is exactly what we were talking about yesterday evening on our drive to the cinema wasn't it?

MC It was it was, how funny you should mention it.

1 How funny.

MC Crumpet?

3 Ta.

MC Right, great. Well, thanks everyone. I think we really got to the bottom of stuff there.

1 We did didn't we?

MC I feel like we've really got a level of understanding now.

5 Mmmm mmm yes understanding, yes that's key.

4 Of course.

3 And listening. Really listening.

2 Of course of course.

MC Well, well done everyone.

2 Good job.

4 That all feels clear.

1 It does.

3 Mm.

5 Cheers.

2 Cheers.

MC Brilliant stuff. Cheers.

They all clink their tea cups and grin. After a second the MC pulls out a gun and shoots each of the characters in the head. The atmosphere changes completely, it is now riotous, celebratory – the best Friday night there ever was. The MC is master of it all, she is a shapeshifter, able to be whatever the night requires. Under her watch everything we see and hear is intoxicating and dangerous.

The Cabaret Begins

(Spoken.) Fuck it. Let's not do that. Let's not talk about
Westminster or Boris or Brussels 'cos we've heard enough
about that. Tonight let's talk about us. Here. 'Cos we're the bit
that matters, aren't we?

I stand here before you tonight to look you in the eye and ask;

(Sung.) What *really* happens?
When a desolate island defined by what it was decides to
delegate to its descendants the chance to redesign its destiny?
What *really* happens?
When a sickly city mocked, shamed, forgotten, deprived and
disposed is given the chance to prove it's been misdiagnosed?
What *really* happens?
When the people so regularly suffocated, raised on severity,
shackled by austerity come up for air, poke their heads out to
see what's still there?

As the MC sings our true setting is revealed – a karaoke bar in the middle of Hull.

So welcome
To our play
Oh you're welcome
To our karaoke cabaret
Where everything is a strange kind of beautiful
And everything is a strange kind of fine
Tonight in a Northern city by the name of Hull
Stands a karaoke bar in the middle of town
Where never-heard souls make never-known plans
Amidst broken bottles and empty roads
In search of a place to finally call home
It's here in this bar by the interchange
Where the whole entire world will change.
I am your camera, your filter through
A forgotten city being born anew

(Spoken.) Tonight we're gunna talk about what runs in this city's hearts and veins and what's threaded through our skin. About hope and resilience and love and humour and cheap pints and bad carpets and grey skies and swagger on a Saturday night and women holding each other like goddesses in pub toilets.

About how, Hull, city of my heart, city of defiance and contradiction, we have started to pull each other apart, and about how wide those cracks seem to have become.

Tonight we're gunna go back and look at where that began for a small group of people in a little karaoke bar in the centre of town.

Tonight we're gunna try and figure out who we are and how we got here and how the fuck we all keep going.

Our story starts eleven years ago on the 24th May 2008, Play-off Final Day.
Welcome, to the best day of our lives.

Act One

SONG – A Sea of Black and Amber

(Our MC throws Hull City scarves, posters, banners and tiger masks out to the audience who create a sea of black and amber. The rest of the cast burst onto the stage with an excited energy, singing and transforming the space, taking us back to that day in 2008...)

ALL
A sea of black and amber and black and amber and black and amber
A sea of black and amber and black and amber and black and amber

And hope in my heart that today might be the day
A change is gonna come
A change is gonna come

MC
2008. The world is in the middle of a building shit storm and Hull's weathered its fair share. But this summer a feeling has been ballooning in this city right and it's been a while but we think we might all recognise it as hope.

As a great big ball of fuck you hope that's built over the last few months with each goal we've scored and each time we've cheered and today the whole city is pulsing with it, up and down.

Because today Hull are gunna beat Bristol City at Wembley and make it into the Premier League.

Because today we're gunna put two fingers up at the rest of the country.

Because today this number one *Crap Town* (2003) doesn't yet know if we'll make it but we're drunk on the headiness of the possibility we even could.

And why are we starting here? Why does today matter?

Because there is a thread that ties together hope and fear and this city has spent its life dangling from the edge of it.

Because hope is dangerous alright, because if you dare to hope, if you dare to dream, then you've further to fall.

And right now hope is growing, right now we're on the cusp ready to explode. And you need to know what that feels like to be able to understand what happens when it's gone.

(Music starts to grow underneath the speech...)

Nowhere can you feel it more than in my bar. Which is rammed and waiting with faces new and old. And it's right here that we first meet our heroes. Drumroll please.

(STEPH is illuminated in the spotlight.)

Steph. 16 years old.
Humber born and Humber bred, strong in the arm and strong in the head.
Born off Greenwood Ave, she's spent all her life in the same postcode.
Her karaoke tune of choice, Bon Jovi, 'You Give Love a Bad Name'/

STEPH sings lines from 'You Give Love a Bad Name' by Bon Jovi.

MC
(Spoken.) Cheers Steph.

(Sung.) Steph has been raised on low expectations,
There's no pressure on her from her relations
School was fine most of the time
And home was fine most of the time
And Steph is fine
most of the time
most of the time
most of the time\

14

She's coasted through life without having to make a choice
Now for the first time she's having to find her own voice
But clocks tick and time turns,
Seas change and candles burn,
Steph hopes and hopes and hopes
That today might be the day
A change is gonna come
LET'S GO

STEPH
(Spoken to the beat, still stood in her spotlight.)
Sixteen years of making do,
Sixteen years of getting by
Sixteen years in this Crap Town
Bringing my aspiration, ambition down
But if the city can dream then so can I
If the city can win then why can't I
Maybe today's the day I start again
I'm filling my head with 'what if' and 'when'
The difference between now and then
When this city started to dream again
Believe again
See the chance to achieve again

'Cos
We're on our way to Wembley
With dreams of what this can be
Of tigers, tigers burning bright
Into the Premier League
The hands on the clock go round and round
My heart bursting through my chest
I'm with my Mum and Dad and Tara
There's no-one else I need
This is about more than football
This is about all of us, City 'til we die
(Arm in arm singing with the MC.) 'Til we fucking die

ALL
A sea of black and amber and black and amber and black and amber
A sea of black and amber and black and amber and black and amber
And hope in my heart that today might be the day
A change is gonna come
A change is gonna come

MC
(With a click the MC stops the action.) Drumroll.
(Anna steps into the spotlight.)
Anna. 18 years old.
Born in Masuria, in Poland, but has the misfortune, or fortune
to find herself tied to us all the same. Song she's always ready to
whip out: 'Prawy Do Lewego' – Kayah & Bregovic.

ANNA W dużej sali duży stół
A przy nim gości tłum
Gospodarz zgięty wpół
Bije łychą w szklanę

MC Lovely Lovely.
(Sung.)
Today Anna's come straight from the station,
Her first time in our strange little nation
To surprise her brother Michal
who's been here since 2004

MICHAL
Working hard on the factory floor
On the same production line as my new wife
Striving, grafting, preparing for family life.

MC. Michal's a man of few words, apart from in the bar back
home where his tune of choice is 'Otwieram Wino' – Sidney Polak.

MICHAL Otwieram wino ze swoją dziewczyną,
chciałbym żeby ten czas nie przeminął.
Otwieram wino ze swoją dziewczyną,
chciałbym żeby ten czas nie przeminął, nigdy
nie przeminął, nigdy nie przeminął.

MC Nailed it.

Hull is not exactly what Anna expects,

But she's ready to embrace whatever comes next

All she wants before she starts at Uni is a few months carefree

To experiment with who exactly, with a little space, she might like to be

For clocks tick and time turns,

Seas change and candles burn,

Anna hopes and hopes and hopes

That today might be the day

A change is gonna come

LET'S GO

(Still in her spotlight ANNA speaks with an intense excitement.)

ANNA

Eighteen and I just don't care

Here to break free of my hometown's glare

I've got all the right answers and all the right words

And I'm finally in a place where they might be heard

Eighteen years to outgrow my home

To be taken hold of by the need to roam.

To find myself, design myself

Finally tell the world how I define myself.

I surprised my brother in his new abode

A shared apartment on Beverley Road

The hands on the clock go round and round

My heart bursting through my chest

I'm here to party in this strange little city

Today's about some kind of football

Today's about all of us, city 'til we die (yeah?)

(Arm in arm, being welcomed by the MC) 'Til we fucking die

ALL

A sea of black and amber and black and amber and black and amber

And hope in my heart that today might be the day

A change is gonna come

A change is gonna come

The Football Match (Part One)

The song ends with a big roar from everyone on stage. Gradually it fades out until it is just ANNA on the table chanting to a bemused MICHAL.

ANNA COME ON THE TIGERS.
You know what I don't understand? Why have we gone from one place to the other to the other? Your friend from work said this was the English way but I would just like to drink and also to sit down. In the last bar I didn't even finish.

Ej, serio wiesz czego nie rozumiem? Czemu ciągle chodzimy od jednego miejsca do drugiego? Twój kumpel z pracy mowił, że to jest w angielskim stylu, ale wolałabym jednak móc usiąść I się napić. W tej ostatniej knajpie nawet nie miałam czasu dokończyć mojego piwa.

She hiccups.

MICHAL Anna, could you, do you have to be so loud?
Anka mogłabyś, mogłabyś nie mówić tak głośno?

ANNA What?
Ale o co Tobie chodzi?

MICHAL Some of these people, I work with.
No niektórzy z tych ludzi to ludzie z mojej pracy.

ANNA Yes.
No i?

MICHAL So maybe you could, you know be a little less/
No więc może spróbuj, spróbuj się jakoś opanować.

ANNA Less?
Opanować?

MICHAL It doesn't matter.
No nieważne.

ANNA OK, OK, I will be very quiet. I will even get off the table.
OK, OK spoko, będę cichutko jak mysz pod miotłą. Patrz, nawet schodzę ze stołu

MICHAL Thank you.
Wielkie dzięki.

ANNA These are the people you work with?
Czyli to są ludzie z którymi pracujesz?

MICHAL Some of them.
Niektórzy.

ANNA Wow. Hull is, it is not what I was expecting. You are very bad at explaining.
Wow. Hull jest , no nie jest tu tak jak sobie wyobrażałam. Opisywanie miejsc nie jest twoja mocną stroną.

MICHAL What?
Ale, o co ci chodzi?

ANNA I mean this could be anywhere. Where is *England*? You know, where is James Bond and gentlemen and women with bonnets and apple trees.
Tak naprawdę moglibyśmy być gdziekolwiek. Gdzie jest ta prawdziwa Anglia? Wiesz o co mi chodzi, James Bond, gentelmeni, kobiety w kapeluszach i pełno drzew, zieleni

MICHAL That's not what you were expecting.
Czyli spodziewałaś się czegoś innego.

ANNA Well no, OK but maybe a little. I didn't think it would be so, so/
No nie, OK może trochę. Na pewno nie myślałam, że tutaj będzie tak...tak...

MICHAL Grey.
Szaro.

ANNA Dirty.
Brudno.

MICHAL There is a park near the flat we will find you a tree.
Niedaleko mojego mieszkania jest taki park, znajdziemy ci jakieś drzewko...

ANNA Thank you.
Dziękuję.

MICHAL Although if it's trees you want you could have stayed at home.
Ale tak an serio jeśli tak bardzo potrzebujesz drzew to mogłaś przecież zostać w domu.

ANNA Yes yes, plenty of trees and beautiful lakes and nothing else yes? It's OK, Hull is, Hull is not rosy but maybe I can grow to like it. For instance I like this man with his belly out watching the tele/
Tak, tak...drzewa, jeziora...no i nic poza tym!
OK, Hull to, no Hull nie jest krainą mlekiem i miodem płynącą, ale może mi się uda jakoś polubić to miasto. Na przykład już lubię tego gościa z brzuchem co się gapi w telewizor......

MICHAL Anna/ *Anka*

ANNA Yes, yes, I like that I don't know anyone/
Tak, tak, wiesz podoba mi się to, to że tak naprawdę nikogo tu nie znam

MICHAL I do/
Ja znam/

ANNA And no one knows me and really it feels like no one will give a shit what we do as long as we're excited for the match. Right? It feels a bit like anything could happen right? Well not anything but something at least right? Something. Right?
I nikt mnie nie zna i naprawdę czuję, czuję, że wszyscy mają gdzieś co tu robimy dopóki jesteśmy tutaj żeby cieszyć się tych ich meczem. No powiedz, nie mam racji? Czuję, że wszystko się może zdarzyć. No może nie wszystko, ale COŚ. Prawda?

MICHAL It could with you here.
No z Tobą tutaj...

ANNA Exactly, so do you want another drink?
Właśnie! To co chcesz kolejne piwo?

MICHAL I've work in the morning /
  Rano do pracy muszę iść /

ANNA And?
  No i?

MICHAL And so do you.
  Ty też!

ANNA What?
  Jak to?

MICHAL They said you could have temporary hours, the
agency, if you come with me in the morning.
  *Powiedzieli w agencji, że Tobie też jakieś tam godziny
  dadzą, jeśli rano ze mną przyjdziesz.*

ANNA Oh great. That's really great. Isn't it? We should have
a drink to celebrate, hey.
  *O świetnie! Super wieści, co nie? Powinniśmy się napić
  żeby to uczcić, hej!!*

MICHAL Let's just watch the game.
  A możemy po prostu obejrzeć ten mecz.

ANNA Are you annoyed I'm here?
  Jesteś wkurzony, że tu jestem?

—

Come on, I couldn't have another summer at home. You know
how it is.
I can't spend all that time hanging around with nothing to do but
pretend to Mama I fancy Dawid… Michal? Come on you know
how Mama is.
  *Sam wiesz, że nie mogłam spędzić kolejnych wakacji w
  domu. Wiesz jak jest. Nie mogę marnować ciągle czasu
  i udawać przed mamą, że kręci mnie Dawid…Michał?
  Przecież sam wiesz jaka mama potrafi być.*

MICHAL Anna/ *Anka?*

ANNA What? *Tak?*

MICHAL You're going back after the summer? *Ale po wakacjach wracasz?*

ANNA For Uni yes. *Zaczynam studia, tak.*

MICHAL And you'll come to work? *I jutro idziesz ze mną do pracy?*

ANNA I said so didn't I, yes. *Przecież powiedziałam, że tak.*

—

Michal? Are you? *Michał? Jesteś wkurzony, że tu jestem?*

MICHAL I could never be annoyed you've come.
 Jak wkurzony? Jak mogę być wkurzony tym, że tu jesteś!

She gives him a hug.

Hey, hey I'm watching the game.
 Ej, ej, próbuję oglądać mecz.

ANNA OK OK I get it, you're watching the game. This is a serious business.
 OK, OK, rozumiem, oglądasz mecz. Poważna sytuacja!!!

She leaps back on the table.

COME ON THE TIGERS!

The Football Match (Part Two)

MC And just across the bar is Steph, along with her mum, Sheila, who loves a bit of Robbie, 'Angels'/

SHEILA sings lines from 'Angels' by Robbie Williams.

MC She's pissed up in a way that only a mum can manage. Steph's best mate, Tara, who'll always blast out Girls Aloud/

TARA sings lines from 'Sound of The Underground' by Girls Aloud.

MC And is preening with all the weight of being sixteen and carrying an attitude which she says makes her grown up and Sheila says makes her a gobshite. And finally her dad, Neil, who likes to throw out a bit of The Jam/

NEIL sings lines from 'Town Called Malice' by The Jam.

MC And who, for one day only, is refusing to be broken by the fact that after thirty years he's just been made redundant from a job he loved by a company who couldn't care less, but is stood barrel-chested in his shirt and shouting:

NEIL We're gunna do it. Already I just know we're gunna fucking do it.

MC And no one tells him to shut up. Instead they're all clinging onto each other, swaying on my dancefloor and at the top of their voices they're:

EVERYONE Singing I love City 'til I die/ Singing I love City 'til I die/ Singing I love City/ I love City/ I love City 'til I die.

STEPH Do you ever get the feeling like this might be the moment we're gunna remember for the rest of our lives? This is like the moment probably that's gunna be mentioned in speeches on our wedding day 'cos nothing could ever top it. Properly like no taking the piss, this is history innit.

TARA Alright Sparticus.

STEPH I'm just saying/

TARA If you talk about football on my wedding day I'm gunna have to punch you in the face.

SHEILA She's got a point Steph.

STEPH No I just mean that/ it's

TARA Unless it's because I'm marrying James Baker, who happens to be watching this match in here today, and it's a cute story about how we met, and how I grabbed him in the heat of the moment and snogged his face off in a totally inappropriate manner.

SHEILA I'm gunna pretend I didn't hear that.

TARA Sorry Sheila, but if you saw him you'd understand.

NEIL An' I'm gunna pretend I didn't hear that.

TARA Sorry Neil!

NEIL You're right though Steph. Hull's never been within a sniff of the Premier League before. But we're on the up, we're gunna do this I can feel it in my bloody bones.

TARA That's just age Neil.

NEIL Oi you. I might have been thrown on the scrapheap by the factory but I aren't that old.

STEPH Dad you haven't been / thrown

TARA No I didn't mean to, I mean I'm sorry about your job and everything / I just

NEIL Course you are, it's fine love I was just taking the piss eh, you gotta laugh haven't you.

TARA I'm sure you'll / get

SHEILA Course he will, years of experience he's got hasn't he /

NEIL Meaning I'm ancient eh /

SHEILA Meaning you're valuable, not many people have been a manager that long have they /

NEIL Meaning I'm expensive 'cos I'm not gunna work for nowt /

SHEILA Yeah well I'm sure you won't have to.

TARA I can't believe they cut everyone.

NEIL Happening all over innit not just us.

TARA It's shit.

SHEILA Yeah, not gunna dwell on it today though are we eh?

STEPH No.

NEIL No. 'Cos today we're gunna bloody smash it!

STEPH COME ON THE TIGERS!

NEIL This could be it you know Steph. Hull, Hull in the Premier League, that'll mean big things.

TARA Yeah?

STEPH It'll mean people have to sit up and take notice won't it?

NEIL It'll mean money Steph, big money coming in. This could be what turns things around.

TARA Oh fucking hell they're coming out.

STEPH and NEIL Oooohhhhhhhhhhhhhhhhh. Come on.

STEPH I can't breathe I'm too nervous.

NEIL *She'll be wearing black and amber when she comes. She'll be wearing black and amber when she comes.*

STEPH and NEIL *She'll be wearing black and amber/ Wearing black and amber*

STEPH, SHEILA, NEIL and TARA *Wearing black and amber when she comes.*

Football Match (Part Three – All)

MC And it's not long before our two heroes meet, finding themselves side-by-side in the crowd, breathing each moment of the match together. Because that's what you do innit? When you're being carried along on a wave of alcohol and hope and blinding excitement.

Because in the air today there is something that is magic, and Anna and Steph can sense in the other something they each need.

STEPH Pass it, pass it.

ANNA Wahhhhhh. No.

STEPH Nearly bloody nearly.

TARA What did you say your name was again?

ANNA Anna.

TARA Right. Welcome to the crew Anna.

STEPH Don't say crew Tara.

TARA We'll slot you right in, although you've got some catching up to do. We've been best mates, since we was four/

STEPH Yeah she dun't need to/

TARA Our mam's found us naked in the garden/ trying to

STEPH Tara I'm not sure she needs to hear that story.

TARA Oh, right, yeah sorry.

ANNA It's OK.

TARA So how come you're here then?

ANNA I'm just/

TARA 'Witnessing history' as Steph's dad will tell you.

NEIL Witnessing but not hearing unless you pipe down and keep your eyes on the ball.

STEPH and TARA We are.

TARA Poland's not exactly round the corner is it. You moved here then?

STEPH Tara/

TARA What?

STEPH It's rude to ask that isn't it, she / might be

TARA It's isn't. It's not rude is it?

ANNA I'm just here because I finished my exams, I have the summer before I go to University, I thought you know–

TARA No?

ANNA Maybe it would be fun, you know, have a little party, earn some money.

TARA So you came to Hull?

STEPH Hey, it's alright here, we know how to party.

TARA Alright we might like a drink Steph but it's hardly Ibiza is it.

ANNA My brother works here.

TARA Oh right. Is that who you're out with then?

STEPH Waahahhhaa

NEIL Defend then, come on.

STEPH Yes!

NEIL Did you see that Steph? Bloody beautiful.

STEPH Yeah!

ANNA Yes. He's just at the bar.

TARA Oh yeah. How old is he?

ANNA What?

TARA Your brother.

ANNA Oh, he's twenty-five.

TARA Oh cool. Yeah everyone thinks I'm about that age.

STEPH Tara /

TARA Is he, single?

STEPH What happened to James Baker?

TARA Just asking.

ANNA He's married.

TARA Oh right. Happily?

STEPH Tara!

NEIL Hey up Deano's getting into gear, where's your mum Steph?

TARA Steph's mum fancies Dean Windass.

STEPH She doesn't really.

NEIL She does, even though he's bout sixty.

TARA He's younger than you isn't he Neil/

NEIL Watch it.

STEPH Dad says he dun't mind 'cos he's one of our own.

NEIL Too bloody right he is let's see what he's gunna do here eh.

TARA Nowt by the looks of that. Right I might just head to the bar then /

STEPH Oh yeah. Might you.

TARA Get us a top up. Anna? Steph? Shots on me.

STEPH You won't get served.

TARA In here? Don't be stupid.

She heads off to the bar.

STEPH Sorry she's a bit /

ANNA She's fun.

STEPH Yeah.

–

So what are you going to do, at Uni I mean what are you going to study.

ANNA Media and Journalism

STEPH Oh right, wow. That sounds, great.

SONG – Heart Skips a Beat

STEPH And she's just sat talking shit like
During the game
And I don't wanna be rude
Make her feel like she's gonna intrude
And there's something nice and something sparking
As she's talking about some course she's gonna be starting
the blood in my veins is pumping, dancing, beating, demanding
I do or say whatever I like and I think I just might
Say something, or
Do something, but for now I just
Keep smiling and keep on listening

ANNA And I'm just sat talking shit like
nothing much to it

29

but deep down inside
something in me feels alive,
as I talk too much explaining my course
I feel this irresistible gravitational force
Pulling me forward, controlling my thoughts
That no-one cares what I am or I'm not
I can do or say whatever I like and I think I just might
Say something, or
Do something, but for now I just
Keep chatting and keep on talking

BOTH
And now we're
both chatting
Fast my heart is pumping
With a
Ba-Boom Boom Boom
Then it skips a beat
And a Ba-Boom Boom Boom
Then it skips a beat

And suddenly we're back in the room
And I remember to breathe
And I remember to breathe
And I remember to breathe
And then,

A silence between them.

say something

A beat.

ANNA Sorry that's probably more than you wanted to know/

STEPH No/

ANNA I didn't mean to/

STEPH No it's really interesting.

ANNA I can get a little bit, my brother always laughs at me, he says not everyone wants to hear the full course outline.

STEPH No it's, it's nice. When you're talking about it your face does this thing it's/

ANNA What

STEPH It's just nice. Sorry that's/ weird

ANNA No. It's like you and your Dad when you talk about football.

STEPH What?

ANNA Your face does this thing.

STEPH Oh right, it's just a big, it's probably stupid it just this is a really big game and/ we've been

ANNA No it's nice. It's a little thing here. *(She touches her cheek.)*

BOTH Ba-Boom Boom Boom
Then it skips a beat

MC And there's something in that moment which is just a bit too much and means they both have to turn and watch the telly, side by side, so aware of that inch of air between them.

And that's how they stay. All waiting, hoping. Until the 38th minute, just before half time when suddenly we hear/

STEPH, NEIL and TARA Deano's unmarked.

MC And we just know something is about to break.

Our MC assumes the role of DEAN WINDASS and slowly and beautifully the rest of the cast begin to lift her as she begins recreating the volley.

SONG – The Sweetest Volley

DEAN WINDASS (MC)
Never done anything as good as this

STEPH
Never felt anything as much as this

DEAN WINDASS (MC)
Every sinew slowly lifts

TARA
The sweetest volley Deano hits

DEAN WINDASS (MC)
Slowly and quickly in the blink of an eye

STEPH
Alcohol rains in the blink of an eye
Arms wrap round in the blink of an eye

TARA
Me and Steph, Sheila and Neil

ANNA / STEPH
My heart beating through my chest

ALL
Ba-boom boom boom
Ba-boom boom boom Screaming shouting blink of an eye
(All.)
CITY TIL WE FUCKING DIE

DEAN WINDASS (MC)
In the blink of an eye
An entire city grows
Changes, evolves, develops, grows
Out of the shadows and into the light
Proof this city is up for the fight
No more Crap Town, no more jokes

Breathing, pulsing, cheering as one
The new beginning has begun
(She takes off her Deano costume, slower.)

The sweetest volley Deano hits

Never felt as good as this…

The scene then explodes.

ALL *WINDASS. YEAAAAAAAHHHSSSSSS.*

STEPH He scores. Course he scores.

EVERYONE OH WHEN THE HULL/ GO MARCHING IN/ OH WHEN THE HULL GO MARCHING IN/ I WANNA BE IN THE NUMBER/ WHEN THE HULL GO MARCHING IN.

MC And somehow in the heat of that moment, in the leaping and joy and movement and just the pure energy of it Anna and Steph find themselves face to face and suddenly they are alone– I mean obviously not literally alone– but suddenly they *feel* alone–

They feel electric–

And in that moment there is a freedom they've both been longing for where they just–

ANNA and STEPH snog.

MC Ba-fucking-boom.

TARA CITY CITY CITY. Yahhhsssshshshshshs. Steph, Steph this is it, this is–
Steph…fucking hell.

NEIL Where is she?

TARA There?

33

NEIL Where?

TARA There, snogging the face off our new best mate.

ANNA and STEPH stop snogging and look at everyone.

Pause.

NEIL Oi, Steph if you're finished could you come here please.

STEPH Dad/

NEIL Now.

She walks over.

NEIL We've bloody dunnit! Deano's bloody dunnit! 104 years of history, this is what we've been dreaming about.

He picks her up and swings her round.

MC And Anna looks across at her brother because she is back in the room now and the weight of what's just happened sits on her, and she isn't sure really, she isn't sure if she's fucked it but she looks at him and after a pause he just says:

MICHAL Now I know why you didn't fancy Dawid.
Teraz już wiem czemu Dawid Ci się nie podoba.

MC And gives this little smile, and that's not much but it's enough.

ANNA grabs STEPH's hand again.

The slowing of time and a tense wait for the final whistle.

SONG – Tick and Tock

ALL Top left corner, the Sky Sports clock
Top left corner, the slowest tick tock
39 40
Tick
And
Tock
49 50
Tick
And
Tock
59 60 69 70
Tick tick tock
79 80 89 90
Tick tick tock
90+1 tick tock
90+2 tick tock
90+3 tick tock
90+4…

This mantra continues underneath the MC's speech.

MC And everyone has to wait, to see if this can last, this
feeling, heart in their mouths, belly up down up down all
through the second half they all have to wait but deep down
everyone knows it's happened now, it's happened.

As the chorus reach '90+4' the MC blows a whistle – everyone cheers.

And as soon as the whistle blows the energy in the room just
explodes. And Steph knows this could be the thing that makes
everything that she knows and loves safe, and Anna knows
that she's finally somewhere where there's the space to try out
who she wants to be, and they're wild, like proper pints going
everywhere, arms on arms on arms wild, and they just–

ALL Yahahahhashshshshahaha.

STEPH We've done it. We've fucking done it.

35

NEIL takes his top off and starts swinging it round singing.

ANNA and STEPH snog again.

NEIL You've been mauled by the Tigers / Mauled by the Tigers / You've been mauled by the Tigers.

STEPH Put your top back on you twat.

NEIL I'm the king of the world.

STEPH You're pissed.

TARA Hey not even Sheila's gunna wanna see that hairy chest Neil. Get it back on.

NEIL Come here, come here. Hull in the Premier League. Hull. This is gunna mean big things, this is gunna change everything!

Everyone comes over except ANNA.

And you an' all now you've detached your tongue from my daughter.

STEPH Dad.

NEIL What? I'm embarrassing you? Get here. Alright.

He hugs everyone.

Fucking hell I love you. I fucking love you all.

ANNA and STEPH hold that feeling, almost like they are watching it from the outside with us.

ANNA And in that moment / *I w tym momencie*

STEPH For all of us, that feeling/

ANNA That night/ *Tamtej nocy*

STEPH and ANNA We can do anything. *Możemy wszystko.*

STEPH We can do fucking anything.

SONG – This Will Never Not Have Happened

NEIL
You live and you work and you fight for something
Anything
To be proud of
To hold onto
To keep you going when the world is
Tough

You hold it in and you don't let on that you're struggling
Really struggling
And you're drowning
Really drowning

In the truth of it, the pain of it and the dirt and the dank and
the dust of it
But then
Dean Windass lifts you from the gutter to the stars
Dean Windass lifts you from the gutter to the stars
Dean Windass lifts you from the gutter to the stars

And you're stood in a pub with your wife and daughter
and you see the smile on her face
and suddenly nothing else matters
Like, losing your job doesn't matter
Having no purpose doesn't matter
And growing old doesn't matter
Nothing else matters but this
My Steph
With that smile on her face
And that shirt on her back
And the fact we're here together living this
Whatever comes next and wherever we go
This will never not have happened
Whatever comes next and wherever we go
This will never not have happened
This will never not have happened
And I hold onto that

37

MC
(Foreshadowing.) Hold onto that…

STEPH, ANNA and TARA *(Together, celebrating.)*
Whatever comes next and wherever we go
This will never not have happened
Whatever comes next and wherever we go
This will never not have happened

STEPH
My life starts here, things are gonna get good
If my city can win then why can't I?

ANNA
My life starts here, things are gonna get good
I know who I am and won't pretend anymore

BOTH
A change is going to come!

The MC watches on as the pub continues to celebrate and speaks directly to the audience as the scene fades in the background.

MC Every night I see people come here to sing their hearts out and remember what it's like to *feel* things in a room with other people.

That's what karaoke's about innit? It's about the chance to belt it out, good or bad, to really let loose and wear your heart on your sleeve and pour your soul into a microphone.

It's about the chance to shine, 'cos for one night only you're onstage and you're a bloody popstar aren't you, you're a superstar and we're all here for you.

So we've a break here and we wanna see some of that alright. Grab a drink if you want it, pop to the loo if you fancy. It's you guys on the mic, first up we've got (*person from the audience*), take it away.

*There is a short break. The bar is open and the audience sing two karaoke songs.

38

ACT TWO

PROLOGUE

The karaoke bar but it feels a little quieter.

Morning vibes.

We get the feeling the lights are coming up and it's time to clear the dancefloor.

MC
(Sung.) Clocks tick and time turns,
Seas change and candles burn
Four years and four days have passed since that final whistle
1,465 days since Deano's guided missile
28th May 2012.

In a Northern city by the name of Hull
Stands a karaoke bar in the middle of town
Where never-heard souls make never-known plans
Where the recession hits hard and compounds our worries
Amidst broken banks and empty Woolies

And in this time of hardship
The whole entire world will change.
I am your camera, your filter through
A dismantled city and its struggles new

(Spoken.)
This next bit you need to hang in tight for alright. Because we all know that little bubble we're all in, that little balloon of hope in our pub in Hull that day can't last can it?
And it doesn't. 'Cos at some point the rest of the world catches up.

There is change, but it's the sort of change you can't control. The sort of change that happens to you and leaves you caught in a trap. The sort of change that makes things feel a bit like they're spinning and spinning and spinning and suddenly you're not in control anymore.

39

SONG – Any Day Now

(Sung.) This change traps and suffocates,

Sees hopes dissipate
Stores shutting and high streets haemorrhaging.
And grey clouds give way to grey days
Grey days expand and our heroes are starting to live in grey ways
Letting their minds wander through the dark
Every now and then back to that day when things felt good
Like anything could happen and that they could do anything

CHORUS
Through the cracks
something good will come
In our town
something pure must come
From the grey
Any day now any day now
Holding onto
any any day now

(ANNA appears with a suitcase and is lit by the spotlight.)

ANNA
Change brings me back to this strange British city
Seeking solace and space, swallow me up British city
Home has my big dreams dampened
Blocked arteries, clogged capillaries.
My coming out locked me in,
a family at war with my admission
Every daily battle diminishing my ammunition
To the point where I have to run
Head down, push on
Fresh start, stay strong.
But still
I hope and hope and hope

Through the cracks
something good will come
In this town
something pure must come
From the grey
Any day now any day now
Holding onto
any any day now

(STEPH appears and is lit by the spotlight.)

STEPH
Change sticks me to the walls of my hometown's rules
It keeps me captive, reactive
Bound to minimum wage for maximum effort
Tied to empty warehouses
Handicapped by bottomed-out bank balances
And centuries-old injustices
I hold onto hope and I fight and I fight
But it's hard to stay standing when reality bites
I'm a cog in a machine that's just not working
A life spent lurking, shirking,
the money I make only growing someone else's earnings
Telling myself

Through the cracks
something good will come
In our town
something pure must come
From the grey
Any day now any day now
Holding onto
any any day now

MC
Together they remember that night and how it felt
To be part of a community that believed in itself
To sing in a crowd where anyone was allowed.

41

Together they hold onto that and the feeling fuels them
Feeds them, drives them, moves and propels them,
Reminds them what's possible.
Anna looking to find a place she can feel at home,
And Steph searching for a way to feel like she belongs in the
place that she's from.

MC, STEPH and ANNA
Any day now, any any day now
Holding onto any any day now

MC 2012. Anna's back. Clutching a newly minted degree in
Media and a mattress on the floor of her brother and his family's
flat.

Because she took the opportunity of graduating to tell her parents,
in that strange way anyone who is gay has to, that maybe she
loves in a different way to the one they had presumed.

And how her parents react leaves her twisted in a way she knew
it would and hoped it couldn't, and sends her to her brother, and
Hull.

Back to a place she remembers as a summer filled with
possibility, where she might be free to be whoever she dreams
of. Because Michal might be a man of few words but when she
rings him and he hears the note in her voice he says:

MICHAL Anna? Are you ok? Come here, you can always come
here for a bit.
*Ania? Wszystko ok? Słuchaj to przyjedź, możesz zostać jakiś
czas.*

MC And hearing that with no questions asked is exactly what
she needs.

But, building a home in a city which has prided itself on
homogeneity will never be easy. Here it's a different part of her
personality which might leave her in a strait jacket of conformity.

42

Because Anna is about to meet our interviewer Shirley, who's no stranger to karaoke, song of choice 'Believe', Cher.

SHIRLEY sings lines from 'Believe' by Cher.

MC Thanks Shirley. And it's Shirley, in a small office on Beverley Road, who's about to teach Anna what it means to be searching for work after Uni in a place which sees you as a disposable part of the low wage economy.

Act Two

Generic office booth.

ANNA I don't understand.

INTERVIEWER Sorry?

ANNA I'm not clear on what you're saying.

INTERVIEWER I'm just saying that looking at your profile we've selected a portfolio of opportunities we think might suit you best/

ANNA Right.

INTERVIEWER So if you'd like to take a look we can probably set you up with an agency/

ANNA An agency?

INTERVIEWER Yes we normally have a number of spaces available that agencies want filled/

ANNA Yes I've done agency work before/ but

INTERVIEWER Amazing, well I really recommend you take a look at form number three it's for a cleaner immediate start/

ANNA This time I was sort of hoping for something a little more related to my degree, ideally something in/ Media

INTERVIEWER We also have a number of entry level positions on the assembly line at/

ANNA I was hoping for something where I could really engage with digital content you know I / have

INTERVIEWER Can you drive?

ANNA Drive? Er yes I can although I don't have a / car

INTERVIEWER We do normally have a high demand for delivery personnel at / various

ANNA In Poland I worked one summer at a local paper helping with their online presence and I was sort of/ hoping that

INTERVIEWER I mean it's more of a question to you really about how quickly you're/willing

ANNA That's why I was so interested in the job in the window/ because it seemed

INTERVIEWER We find people who are willing to dive straight in and just get on with it have the most success.

ANNA Right.

INTERVIEWER Brilliant. So I'll make a call, you're willing to start tomorrow?

ANNA I'm sorry, doing what?

INTERVIEWER The cleaner wasn't it? That's what you've experience in.

ANNA No. Well yes but that's not what I/ was

INTERVIEWER Fantastic it should definitely be easy to place you, a can-do attitude is so important.

ANNA OK great. That's brilliant, sorry Shirley, right?

INTERVIEWER Yes.

ANNA Yeah that's great Shirley, absolutely fantastic, only thing is I'm still a bit confused/

INTERVIEWER OK.

ANNA Because that's not the job I came into ask about is it, so I'm just wondering why it/ is

INTERVIEWER Well you must understand/

ANNA No sorry, I'm just wondering why it is you've chosen to show them to me when the job I was asking about is in/ digital

INTERVIEWER Well as I said judging from your CV and profile/

ANNA OK. Yes. I'm really interested what it is about my profile made you think these would be what I was interested in?

INTERVIEWER Well looking at your experience I can see/

ANNA I have a degree, top marks.

INTERVIEWER Yes. Of course, well in the current climate/

ANNA I speak two languages.

INTERVIEWER If you were looking at any of our factory floors having English as well would definitely enable you to enter a more desirable position.

ANNA I'd like to look at the job I enquired about from the window.

INTERVIEWER Well that's more of a, a general, rolling job opportunities with that firm you see, and currently we don't, I mean they have a very specific brief/

ANNA I can be specific.

INTERVIEWER Maybe if you were to gain some more experience/

ANNA In my degree we did several internships in the industry and like I said one summer I/ worked

INTERVIEWER Yes. Yes. Newspaper delivery.

ANNA No/ I was

INTERVIEWER That's commendable definitely, it can be difficult in these times, we're all having to take what's on offer/

ANNA I understand that but/

INTERVIEWER Maybe if you were to work a little bit on your, I mean it's going to be hard to place you outside of the traditional, particularly with your accent/

ANNA My accent?

INTERVIEWER We all need to accept where our bracket is in terms of employability.

ANNA I totally understand that but I suppose what I am saying is I feel my qualifications mean/ I could

INTERVIEWER I think that's really for us to decide.

ANNA Is it?

INTERVIEWER Although, if you're sure none of these offers are what you're interested in I do have one other position/

ANNA Great. OK. That's great.

INTERVIEWER It's in catering. Zero-hours contract, all through a very respectable contractor. Lots of excellent client testimonials here as you can see.

ANNA Catering?

INTERVIEWER I'm sure they'd be very keen, we send a lot of, I mean they're normally very happy with people of your, erm, demographic.

ANNA Right. Demographic.

—

INTERVIEWER So shall I send you? I mean it's as part of an events staff, varied hours, minimum wage mostly but variety, I'm sure it will be very…engaging.

ANNA Of course. I already feel very engaged.

INTERVIEWER I mean a lot of people would be very happy to have anything at all currently so don't feel you have/to

ANNA I'll go.

INTERVIEWER Brilliant, I'll give them a ring.

ANNA Fucking brilliant.

SONG – Minimum Wage, Maximum Effort

MC
And as the phone rings and the wheels begin to turn
There is still an important lesson that Anna must learn

INTERVIEWER
There are certain people who do certain things
And other people who do other things
Yes, there are certain people who do certain things

MC
(Like, banking)

INTERVIEWER
And other people who do other things

MC
(Like, cleaning)

INTERVIEWER
Oh, there are certain people from certain places who do certain things

MC
(Like, running the country)

INTERVIEWER
And other people from other places who do other things

MC
(Like, waiting tables)

INTERVIEWER
It's not about the way you sound, I promise
And it's not about the way you look, I swear.
But you can't come here and take our jobs,
And you can't come here and sponge off the state.

Here minimum wage takes maximum effort
Minimum wage takes maximum effort
Oh, and God Save The Queen.

MC
And as the phone is answered and the job's confirmed
There is still an important lesson that Anna must learn.

For clocks tick and time turns,
Seas change and candles burn
And on the other side of the city in a hospital waiting room
Steph's Humber heart is breaking.

SCENE TWO

Hull Royal waiting room.

MC She's not had an easy time since we last saw her. 'Cos her Dad never does get another job. And the wheels of fortune never do land on her or Hull. And instead she just has to watch everyone she loves straining and struggling and pretending that something is just round the corner. Until today she finds herself here, stood in Hull Royal waiting room, where a Doctor whose weekends are spent blasting out Gloria Gaynor/

DOCTOR sings lines from 'I Will Survive' by Gloria Gaynor.

MC Is about to change her life forever.

STEPH I don't understand.

DOCTOR I'm very sorry.

STEPH No, mum, please I don't understand.

SHEILA Sit down love.

STEPH No I'm not really sure/

DOCTOR I'm really sorry Steph but like I said to your mum there's nothing else we can do.

STEPH He was only, he was only, this morning he was fine.

SHEILA Steph/

STEPH No Mum, he really was wasn't he?

SHEILA Yes love.

DOCTOR Sometimes, I'm really sorry, with heart disease it's very easy to miss the signs sometimes, and with your father's age and lifestyle/

STEPH He was only fifty fucking four.

SHEILA Steph.

STEPH Lifestyle?

DOCTOR I mean weight, age, exercise they're all factors/ it doesn't

STEPH You think he's dead because of a few bacon sarnies.

DOCTOR Look all I'm trying to say is it's no one's fault. I really, I am very sorry.

STEPH It is someone's fault.

SHEILA Steph please.

STEPH No it is though isn't it. If he'd have seen him these past few years he wouldn't be saying it's no one's fault. If he'd have seen him having to get the bus to the job centre after the factory closed/

SHEILA Steph there's no point/

STEPH No he would though wouldn't he? Every morning on that fucking bus. And you could see it, you could see it in his face it was making it like he couldn't breathe, like it was clogging up his arteries and his throat and he was just having to push it all back in he was just having– Like the shame of it he was just having to– Fuck.

I bet that's what–

SHEILA Steph/

STEPH Fuck. He was fine this morning, he–

I called you, as soon as I got back from work I found him and I called you and I thought if the ambulance came, I thought–

DOCTOR I'm really sorry we have tried, we've really tried but he can't be resuscitated.

—

I'm going to give you ten minutes OK. And then I'm going to come back and see what you'd like to do. Just take your time.

—

SHEILA Oh fucking hell Steph. Oh fucking hell. Oh fucking, oh. Please.

STEPH runs to her and they hug in the middle of the room for a long time.

STEPH What are we gunna do now Mum?

51

—

SHEILA I dunno I, I think we just sit love.

STEPH OK.

SHEILA We sit and we wait until we're ready and then we go in and say goodbye.

STEPH I didn't think–

SHEILA Yeah.

—

STEPH Remember that day the other summer, at the match, when he smeared that pickle sandwich all round his face/

SHEILA Victory paint/

STEPH I didn't think he would ever/

SHEILA No.

STEPH He seemed fine. He seemed/

SHEILA Yes.

STEPH This isn't meant to happen. Like, this isn't meant to happen yet.

—

SHEILA If they could see what they've done to him. If they could–

He couldn't have carried on Steph. He's shrunk, an inch in the last six months. I'm not joking, I've had to take his trousers up/

—

STEPH Mum I don't want him to go.

SHEILA Me neither love. Me–

They cry and hold each other again.

SHEILA Bacon fucking sarnies.

—

STEPH What do we do now?

SHEILA We say goodbye and we tell him we love him.

STEPH OK.

SHEILA OK.

STEPH Fuck OK.

SHEILA And then we'll–

We'll–

Fuck we'll–

—

STEPH We'll just get on with it won't we. 'Cos that's what you have to do init, get on with it.

We'll know though. We'll know who's fault it is. And we won't ever forget.

SONG – This Will Never Not Have Happened (reprise)

STEPH
You live and you work and you fight for something
Anything
To be proud of
To hold onto

53

To keep you going when the world is
Tough

You hold it in and you don't let on when you're struggling
Really struggling
When you're drowning
Really drowning
In the truth of it, the pain of it and the dirt and the dank and
the dust of it
But then

STEPH and NEIL
Dean Windass took us from the gutter to the stars
Dean Windass took us from the gutter to the stars
Dean Windass took us from the gutter to the stars

STEPH
Now I'm here in Hull Royal with my warrior Mum
and I miss the smile on his face
and suddenly nothing else matters
Like, having a shit job doesn't matter
And having no purpose doesn't matter
And having no plan doesn't matter
Nothing else matters but this
But Dad
My Dad
With that smile on his face
And that shirt on his back
And the fact we were together living it
And I think
Whatever comes next and wherever we go
This will never not have happened

STEPH and NEIL
Whatever comes next and wherever we go
This will never not have happened
This will never not have happened

STEPH
And I hold onto that.

(Dreamlike, the stage transforms into the wake.)

SCENE THREE

The pub, STEPH's dad's wake. Everyone is a bit drunk and morose. ANNA is here waitressing with the catering company.

SONG – Now They're All Wearing Black

MC
Now they're all wearing black
And they remember the good old times
Like when Neil did this, and when Neil said that
When Neil got sunburnt on his pale white back
When he woke up the kids dropping Santa's sack
When he proposed to Sheila on a beach in Greece
When he had that run-in with the French police

STEPH
And now we're all wearing black
To say goodbye, to remember
To pay our respects and to never forget
But the memories are different now,
filtered by finality, confined to the past
A fractured retelling of how he told the story last

MC
Now they're all wearing black

CHORUS
To raise a glass for one last time
To reminisce about the good old times
Now we're all wearing black
Now we're all wearing black

MC

And they laugh and they sob
And they hold on tight
And they think all the things they keep deep down
And they're all wearing black

STEPH

My dad was my hero and I never will forget
All the things that he did and the words that he said
He was one of a kind and I never will forget

I'll keep him close and I'll make him proud
Oh Dad
My Dad

CHORUS

So raise a glass for one last time
To reminisce about the good old times
Now we're all wearing black
For you we're all wearing black

TARA Are you alright? I mean, yeah sorry that's stupid, I just mean–

STEPH Yeah.

TARA OK.

—

Hey, at least the funeral director was a bit dreamy wanna he, at least /

STEPH Tara.

TARA Sorry, I'm joking, obviously I'm /

STEPH Can you just–

TARA Yeah. Yeah course. Sorry.

—

Free bar's a bit dangerous innit.

STEPH Mam's idea–

TARA Thought it might be.

STEPH Yeah.

TARA Love your mam.

STEPH Yeah.

TARA I've missed you. I would've come round or, I wasn't sure if you just wanted to–

STEPH No me neither really.

TARA Have you been off work?

STEPH Yeah for a bit they said/

TARA Great, I mean that's really good I think/

STEPH Yeah, maybe. I dunno, just sat round now though aren't I.

—

TARA Have you thought anymore, like have you thought anymore about coming back to college 'cos some people were asking/

STEPH I dunno/

TARA Just I could take the form in for you, if you want, or like get mam to do it when she's on reception.

STEPH I dunno Tara it's not really top of my list right now.

TARA Yeah, no, course I just/

STEPH I'm not really thinking about it.

TARA Yeah I just thought, well I just knew you were thinking you might next year and I didn't want this to stop you. Like I just mean you shouldn't not get a chance to do stuff 'cos of this should you? And I mean A-levels are like, important aren't they /

STEPH You've changed your tune.

TARA Yeah well you know what I mean they are though aren't they? Doing this year again, it's my chance to properly take it seriously innit, and I mean I don't want you to miss out on your chance to get out of here, to leave just 'cos / this has

STEPH Leave?

TARA Yeah just, you know that's our chance, for Uni innit? Not to be stuck here. And if I've done it you could and your Dad wouldn't want you/ to

STEPH I don't wanna leave.

TARA No but I just meant/

STEPH No but why is that always everyone's answer? Why is it always like you're some big failure if you don't dream of fucking off to Leeds like it's the promised land.

TARA I dunno Steph, it's just, it's what you do innit. Like do you still wanna be here in five years, in this bar /

STEPH I love this bar /

TARA Yeah me too mate I just mean /

STEPH This bar is where we had our one and only snog to Katy Perry–

TARA Yeah, one and definitely only.

STEPH It's where we first discovered if you soaked a cigarette in Liquid Gold it felt like your heart was gunna pop.

TARA Because it probably was.

STEPH I'm saying /

TARA I know. I know what you're saying. You're right it's amazing but I just meant, like I dunno, I just meant, I was just checking if there's anything I could do–

STEPH Yeah. Yeah no there isn't 'cos there isn't really is there 'cos nothing's gunna, 'cos he's gone now and nothing's gunna–

TARA Yeah. OK. Sorry.

God Steph I am really fucking sorry.

—

STEPH I just want, I just want everything to stand still for a bit actually. Like I just want us all to be on this dancefloor having a massive laugh, all of us together, just for a bit longer, just to not know he's not coming back, not to know that he's– Oh shit.

TARA Eh come here, come here.

They hug. STEPH is crying a bit.

STEPH Thanks. Thanks. Gin innit.

TARA Yeah.

STEPH Do you want another?

TARA Actually, I'm gunna, well it's, I've got a politics exam in the morning haven't I so I'm just gunna stick to water–

STEPH Oh right. Oh right yeah.

TARA Could get you one though, if you want?

STEPH No. No it's fine.

MC
And Steph sits and she sobs
And she holds on tight
And she thinks all the things we keep deep down
How the memories are different now,
filtered by finality, confined to the past
A fractured retelling of how he told the story last
And she just wants him back
She really just wants him back

SCENE FOUR

Outside. ANNA is stood on her break with a fag. She is on the phone.

ANNA Hi.

So. So you aren't going to answer the phone I get that. And I was going to not speak to you too, I was going to–

Because I am really really angry actually and I think I have the right to be I have–

But. But I'm just ringing to say that, I'm here. And I'm fine. In case you were worried. And Michal said I could stay for a bit in the baby's room which is nice actually, so I'm going to. And I won't be lonely because I think he will always be there for me.

Even if you think I will never have a family like you said.

And I've got a job and it's, well I've got something anyway. And no I'm not coming back to do my Master's yet because–

Because I can't breathe there. I can't.

I think it's all a bit much isn't it? I think it was all a bit much to come home after Uni and just expect us to go back to how we were.

But I just want to say I'm here and I'm fine and I've got a job and I'm going to get a better job and this is my life and it's fine, it's different to how you expected but that's fine.

And I miss you. And Papa and even Grandma and you can tell her I'm not even smoking here because it is so expensive.

She looks at her cigarette.

Well much less, I mean hardly at all anyway so she can be happy. And she doesn't need to keep sending Michal all those huge parcels because there are Polish shops here and they are pretty good, honestly, and you know Pierogi doesn't post so well.

OK. OK. That's all.

That's all except to say I'm not sorry I told you because there is only so long you can pretend even if– Anyway I'm not sorry but I hope you– I hope one day you and Papa can.

Yeah. OK. Right. Right bye anyway.

Cześć.

No, no więc nie odbierasz telefonu, rozumiem to. Prawdę mówiąc planowałam z Tobą nie rozmawiać wcale, planowałam

—

Jestem na Ciebie strasznie, strasznie wściekła i wydaje mi się, że mam prawo być, mam prawo– Ale dzwonię. Dzwonię, żeby Ci powiedzieć, że jestem tutaj i wszystko jest w porządku, więc nie musisz się martwić. Jeśli się martwiłaś. Michał mówi, że mogę zostać na jakiś czas w pokoju małej, to miłe z jego strony, no więc zostanę. Nie czuję się samotna wiedząc, że mogę zawsze na nim polegać.

Więc nawet jeśli myślisz, że nigdy nie będę miała rodziny mam jego.

Mam pracę, także to zawsze coś. I nie, nie wracam, żeby robić magistra, nie teraz, bo–

Nie umiem tam oddychać. Nie umiem.

Może to było dla was zbyt wiele... Wróciłam po studiach i oczekiwałam, że wszystko będzie tak jak kiedyś.

Ale chcę Ci powiedzieć, że jestem tu i wszystko jest w porządku. Mam pracę, będę się starać o jakąś lepszą posadę. To moje życie. Jest inaczej niż się spodziewałaś ale jest dobrze.

Tęsknie za Tobą. Za Tatą też, no i za Babcią. Powiedz jej, że nie palę, tutaj papierosy są strasznie drogie–

She looks at her cigarette.

Palę mniej, tak naprawdę prawie wcale, więc na pewno się ucieszy. Aha, i powiedz jej, że nie musi wysyłać Michałowi tych paczek bo mamy tutaj pełno polskich sklepów, które są dobrze zaopatrzone.

Poza tym pierogi wysyłane pocztą nie smakują najlepiej... OK. OK. No to.... to wszystko.

To wszystko, z wyjątkiem tego, z wyjątkiem tego, że chcę ci powiedzieć, że nie żałuję, że Ci powiedziałam, przyszedł moment w którym miałam dość udawania, nawet jeśli ceną było– każdym razie, nie żałuję, ale mam nadzieję, że–

Mam nadzieję, że pewnego dnia Ty i Tata będziecie mogli Uhm. OK. No. No to do pogadania.

STEPH has come outside and is watching her.

STEPH Sorry were you/

ANNA No. No it's fine.

STEPH OK.

ANNA Just family you know.

STEPH Yeah.

ANNA Yeah, right sorry. Of course.

Offers her a cig.

Do you want one?

STEPH Thanks.

She chokes.

ANNA Do you smoke?

STEPH No, but like just buried my dad so I reckon /

ANNA Fair enough.

They smoke for a bit.

STEPH I dunno if you remember but we er, like the other summer–

ANNA Yeah. Yeah I remember.

STEPH Right. Yeah. Cool.

—

So you stayed then /

ANNA What?

STEPH Here. Like I remember you saying you were just visiting your brother.

ANNA Oh right. Yes I was. No I went back actually.

STEPH Oh right.

ANNA Yes. But I just finished Uni and I'm sort of looking for a job you know, and I thought the money here might be /

STEPH Oh right, course.

ANNA Plus Mum wants me to get married so /

STEPH Right. Not on the top of your list.

ANNA Not yet no. She's not really that cool with the whole sleeping with women thing so–

STEPH Right.

ANNA Yeah. So here I am.

STEPH Fair enough.

ANNA Twenty-two, on my brother's floor. Waitress at a wake. Sorry I didn't mean–

STEPH It's alright.

ANNA Sorry.

STEPH Good to have anything nowadays really I suppose innit.

ANNA Is it?

STEPH Just like, I dunno. Lots of people at the minute have got nowt haven't they.

ANNA Is that what happened to your dad?

STEPH Dunno. Like after he lost his job he like, I dunno it sounds stupid but like he sunk. All of him it sort of–

And he was, for a long time he was sure something was coming but it just, he was old, I suppose no one wants to–

The Job Centre sent him for loads of shit like, just shit they knew he wouldn't or couldn't do– I mean he had pride you know, like before, in what he was doing and he didn't want to just–

They sent him for an interview to be a cleaner once, Mum lost it then, she said he's never cleaned anything in his life, she would know–

Sorry I don't mean, being a cleaner like it's fine I just mean–

ANNA I'm not a cleaner.

STEPH Yeah. Sorry I just meant. Sorry.

ANNA OK.

ANNA finishes her cig and goes to head inside.

STEPH Actually do you think you could / maybe

ANNA Yeah?

STEPH Do you think you could like stay, just for a second. Like I mean could you, could you wait out here with me, just for a bit?

ANNA I'm sort of, my break isn't very long.

STEPH Oh, oh right yeah.

ANNA But maybe…just for a bit I'm sure it will be fine.

STEPH Thanks. Thank you.

ANNA It's OK.

STEPH Sorry I'm just a bit, hot maybe I dunno. I–

Everyone in there, it's a bit. Everyone smiling and talking like he had a great life and touching me and saying they're sorry and nothing anyone could have done and I dunno I don't think that's true is it. And
I just–

ANNA OK.

STEPH Thanks.

—

Sometimes, like sometimes it feels like I'm screaming, all the time I'm screaming on the inside and no one is listening.

—

65

I'm sorry.

ANNA It's OK.

STEPH You probably think I'm crazy.

—

ANNA …You know, that first summer after I got here, after that match, and we, yeah exactly, everything was so–

I had a lot of fun you know. I thought, Hull, OK, maybe this is me.

And going home it was like, I couldn't. Going home I couldn't bring myself to do it, to catch people's faces when I held a girl's hand, or my family, to–

Because where I come from it is a small place you know and people they– There is not always space for people to be different.

So when I finished studying this year I came back. Here. And then you realise people are looking at you for a different reason. When you talk in Polish in the street, or you express an opinion they don't like or whatever.

And don't get me wrong it's not, I am fine. But what I'm saying is I know what it is when people make you feel like you don't matter. When people make you–
And you remember them those people, inside you remember them and you build them up, right you build them until all the things you are shouting at them inside are all the things that build so it's all you can hear in your ears and you are raging.

And you think–

I remember you and one day I will let you know what it feels like to scream and for no one to listen. One day I will let you know rage.

66

STEPH Fuck.

ANNA Yes.

STEPH And then, and then what? Like, and then what do you do?

ANNA What?

STEPH What? With all that, what do you do? Like I'm so angry all the time like what do you do with that, with this fucking grief of stuff happening around me and of no one listening and no one giving a shit, and Dad's face and that moment, that moment when we thought everything might change and actually everyone was fucking laughing at us weren't they, at the thought things could ever be different, that we might change things, everyone was– What do you do with that?

ANNA I don't know. I don't know but fuck I wish I did.

SONG – Something Eternal Burns

STEPH And in that moment we look at each other/

ANNA And we are burning. *I czujemy jak się spalamy*

STEPH Inside we are burning.

ANNA Inside we are/ *W środku*

STEPH and ANNA
AHHHHHGHGHGHGHHHHGHGDSCUNV
FUIFVFUUVNUVNNVAHAHAHUV
FOOVDFIOBBNBNBNBNBNBN.

STEPH and ANNA And no one is there to put us out.
I nikt nie jest w stanie nam pomóc

STEPH
My mind is racing and I'm pacing and
I can't get a grip

Fury fuels me and fights me
It tears and it rips.
They say these streets lay foundations of rage
Was I the only one content in my communal cage?
Now with dad gone, my pillar and rock
I can't understand why everything else
hasn't
just
stopped
But the world keeps on turning and inside I'm burning
Inside I'm burning and I can't, just can't,
I just can't. do. this.

ANNA
Wherever I am and wherever I go
It burns and it burns until its ingrained
This feeling of other, of not being the same
I stand and I smile and I don't give an inch
I will not say sorry, I will not flinch
'Cos inside the fire in my soul rages and roars
It rages and roars and rages and roars
I'm not giving up, something has to change
But the world keeps on turning and inside I'm burning
Inside I'm burning and I can't, just can't,
I just can't. not. fly.

MC
And inside they scream and inside they shout
Their fire is burning and they need it put out
Their foundations are rocked, their dreams ablaze
Each flicker of hope no more than a phase
This world doesn't care about a girl from the North
It doesn't have space for one from the East

So as clocks tick and time turns,
Seas change and candles burn
Something has to change.

Something has to change.
Something has to change.
Because
This
Just
Isn't
IT.

(STEPH and ANNA repeat the verses from before, this time overlapping and intersecting with each other and building towards crescendo.)

ALL
Something eternal burns and it burns
Something inside us all
Something eternal burns
It burns and it burns and it burns
Something so deep
Something so raw

In the stars and the stones and the bricks and our bones
In the sky and the shore and forever more
Something eternal burns and it burns
Something eternal between us all
Something eternal burns
And we know

ANNA and STEPH
There's more than this
There just has to be
Something isn't right
All that we can be

MC
Something eternal burns and it burns
Something searing surging
Sparking burning
Eternal yearning
Something has to change

MC Right. Time to grab another pint. We've got three bangers coming up from (*audience names*) before we rejoin our heroes so time to take a breath, have a piss, lose yourself on the dancefloor, whatever takes your fancy alright, make the most of it 'cos you know what's coming next.

*There is a short break. The bar is open and the audience sing two karaoke songs.

Act Three

MC Wahoooo. Anyone for a top-up? Come on, come on don't be shy.
It's a big night tonight. We're gunna need a drink.
They've got the right idea. Little top up? Tempt you? It's bubbly? Well, Cava. Still it's nice. Yeah. That persuaded you? Brilliant. Alright. Everyone sorted? OK great.

The MC moves into her spotlight.

(Sung.) Clocks tick and time turns,
Seas change and candles burn
Eight years and thirty days have passed since that final whistle
2,952 days since Deano's guided missile
23rd June 2016. The day of the referendum.

Yeah I know, told you you'd need a drink.

(Sung.) In a Northern city by the name of Hull
Stands a karaoke bar in the middle of town
Where never-heard souls make never-known plans
Where the chance to vote has a different weight
Amidst broken dreams and the welfare state
And in this time of hardship
The whole world will change.
I am your camera, your filter through
A divided city and its struggles new

The karaoke bar. Six years later.

SONG – A Dance on a Volcano

Things quickly get into full swing, the rest of the cast enter.

Bang. Suddenly the MC pops two more bottles of Champagne.

She wanders through the audience topping up people's glasses and encouraging the general feeling of a Big Night. She gives out mini Union Jack flags, hats, etc.

ALL
A sea of red and white and blue and red and white and blue
A sea of red and white and blue and red and white and blue

MC
(Spoken.) Hull. My pub. Again. And one more big night out.

Well what a rollercoaster we've been on eh? There's been some difficult years alright. I'm not gunna pretend. But we've got back up, alright? We're used to that aren't we, getting knocked back by everyone right but always getting back up. And it's been hard yeah but also right, they've announced that next year, next fucking year we're gunna be City of Culture.

And some of us are feeling swept up in that, in the excitement about what that might mean. That things are gunna really be different now yeah, that we're gunna get some recognition for all this talent, for the great big beating, thriving, striving, heart that is this city.

And some of us aren't. Yeah, OK 'cos we've been here before.

And if people reckon this is like suddenly a nice place to live now, why is life still so hard?

So here we are, Brexit.

The bit where Steph and Sheila are tired of clinging on, alone, and see a chance to stand up and say they matter. Neil matters. And the future has to make that safe.

72

The bit where Anna and Michal look at the change they've made to a city, with new shops and signs and energy, and question why suddenly people think that's not a positive note in its developing identity.

The bit where everything falls apart and we're not sure how to put it back together again.

(Sung.) Tonight we dance on a volcano
Our toes tingle at the taste
Of something that's new
Of something unknown
Of something unseen
Something that may…
Might just…
Could be…

A sea of red and white and blue and red and white and blue
A sea of red and white and blue and red and white and blue

A city that's split down the middle
A city being tugged at the seams
It may not be London or Paris or Berlin
And that's where this whole thing begins
'Cos our fears are different here
Our fears are different here
It's us against whatever you bring
Her fears are different here
Her fears are different here
It's us against whatever you bring

So, tonight we dance on a volcano
Our toes they tingle at the taste
Of something that's new
Of something unknown
Of something unseen
Something that may…
Might just…
Could be…

ANNA
Still here
Existing here
Finally making a living here
I'm tapdancing, jiving, waltzing
unaware of the coming stumbles
As just below the volcano rumbles,
bubbles, bursts, pops and grumbles

STEPH
Stayed here
Happy here
Never thought about leaving here
I'm hopping, skipping, diving, jumping
unaware of the coming blitz
As just below the volcano spits,
commits, burns, fizzes and licks

ALL
So tonight we dance on a volcano
Our toes they tingle at the taste
Of something that's new
Of something unknown
Of something unseen
Something that may…
Might just…
Could be…

A sea of red and white and blue and red and white and blue
A sea of red and white and blue and red and white and blue

SCENE TWO

MC So Anna's still here. And after a series of shitty and less shitty jobs she's finally got to quit the latest for a step down the road of what she first hoped for after Uni. Digital Marketing Officer for a new start-up company, and that is something to celebrate, which she is trying to do at her leaving do with her work mate, Jordan, who loves a bit of Futureheads on a Saturday night/

JORDAN Oh oh ohhh oh/ The hounds of love are calling/

MC And she is trying to ignore what tonight is, and what it might mean, just like she has been trying to ignore the feeling that's been building and building in this place since the campaign.

ANNA and her work friend are doing shots.

ANNA No more wiping Bethany Knight's bum when she's wet herself again.

JORDAN No more scraping nits out of Lewis Morley's scratty head.

ANNA No more listening to Mrs Robertson's three principles of progression or data days for direct improvement or bum holes for better results/

JORDAN That isn't one.

ANNA Obviously that fucking isn't one.

JORDAN You never know with her.

ANNA No more.

JORDAN No more.

ANNA Cheers.

JORDAN Cheers. Fuck I'm almost jealous.

ANNA You are jealous.

JORDAN I am officially jealous.

ANNA You're pissed.

JORDAN That too.

ANNA Maybe I could employ you as an assistant/

JORDAN You what?

ANNA You could come with me, make my tea, fan me in important meetings/

JORDAN Fuck off.

ANNA You'd have to have a change of attitude.

JORDAN You can make my tea ta very much.

ANNA No, today, today was the day I make my last cup of tea for someone else.

JORDAN Me too.

ANNA Really?

JORDAN Yeah from now on Mrs Robertson can make her own cuppas, I'm making a stand.

ANNA Fuck, wish I was there to see it.

JORDAN Some would say it's a strange hill to die on but I'm committed.

ANNA I salute you.

JORDAN Thanks.

ANNA Cheers.

JORDAN Cheers. God like, honestly Anna I am happy for you though.

ANNA Thanks.

JORDAN No more Springhouse Primary.

ANNA I'll come visit.

JORDAN You won't.

ANNA I will.

JORDAN You better, us T.A.s have a long memory.

ANNA I might even miss you.

JORDAN Yeah.

There are cheers at the TV, some politician is on.

Picked a night for it haven't we.

ANNA No, no no no what was the rule/

JORDAN We don't mention Brex/it

ANNA Ahhhhhh you said it.

JORDAN I only/

ANNA You said it though.

(ANNA makes him take a shot – 'Brexit' is a banned word in their drinking game.)

JORDAN Yeah, sorry, sorry. We'll know won't we anyway soon.

ANNA Know what? No one will know anything I don't think.

JORDAN The papers reckon we're going to remain anyway.

ANNA They can think what they want. I've had five parents in the playground this week tell me it's nothing personal but blah blah blah.

JORDAN Five?

ANNA Yes.

JORDAN Shit.

ANNA Yes.

JORDAN I didn't know we had five parents who could be arsed to pick their kids up/

ANNA Michal is going home.

JORDAN What?

ANNA He, I don't know if it's because of the vote but, there is all this uncertainty you know it is just–

JORDAN Yeah.

ANNA And with little Ewa now, she is starting school soon and I think he just wants her to feel, she won't speak Polish to them you know at home only English and I think he wants to go before it is too hard for her.

JORDAN I'm sorry Anna.

ANNA It's OK. He can get a job, less money but he can have my parents to help with Ewa. The schools there are better, it is probably a good choice.

JORDAN Do you think you would ever?

ANNA Me? I don't know, sometimes I have this feeling in my heart you know Poland is, there is nowhere else like it in the world you know.

JORDAN That's what I thought about Hull last week when that man took a shit down our tenfoot.

ANNA Yeah, no seriously there isn't, but/

JORDAN Yeah?

ANNA I used to think the further you were from something the clearer you see it yes? But now I'm not sure. This feeling, Michal has it too OK but for me I'm not sure it's true, it's a little rose-tinted glasses you know, I don't know if that place in my head is a little made-up.

JORDAN I dunno those pictures you showed us last summer looked pretty rosy.

ANNA Yes, I love to go back to visit yes but. The feeling there actually to live, there are things building there too, you know–

There too I'm just not quite right. I am gorszy sort. No my life is here now, I ran away once already, I'm not going anywhere again unless I want to.

JORDAN Also you'd miss me.

ANNA Maybe/

JORDAN After all your life is here/

ANNA If you're my life then maybe I should leave.

JORDAN Maybe. Is Michal coming tonight then?

ANNA Later he said, he doesn't finish work 'til late.

JORDAN To you. To you and your new job and being very busy and important now.

ANNA Cheers.

JORDAN Cheers. Right, are we gunna do some karaoke or what?

SCENE THREE

MC Today's Steph's birthday. She's here with Tara and Sheila and she's really wants to recreate that feeling that they're all in it together, ready to celebrate what she thinks is her chance to have her say about the nation state. But, although most of the time she thinks she's happy, surrounded by people she knows and places she's comfy, with Tara things are no longer easy, 'cos, ever since she came back from Uni, Steph can't help but feel left behind, thinking her life might seem like a dead end through another's eyes.

Meanwhile, Sheila is really getting into it on the karaoke.

SHEILA This one goes out to my little angel, twenty-four today and ready to see the world change, aren't you Steph love.

She starts singing 'Wonderwall' by Oasis.

TARA God it's really not changed in here at all has it.

STEPH What's that meant to mean?

TARA Nothing, just saying it's the same isn't it. Right down to the carpet.

STEPH There's nothing wrong with that carpet.

TARA I'm not saying there is.

STEPH It was new last year actually.

TARA I'm just saying it's a similiar pattern isn't it then. Similiar vibe.

STEPH And?

TARA And, and nothing. It's nice actually.

STEPH It's not nice it's shit it's always been shit.

TARA Alright it's shit then.

—

STEPH So how long you back for this time?

TARA I dunno. I've sort of finished now, just graduation so a bit I think. Stuck here until I can get a job or something anyway.

STEPH Right.

—

TARA My mum's doing my head in, she can't leave me alone, she followed me into the bathroom this morning, I had to ask her if she wanted to help me take a shit. Dunno how you still live at home.

STEPH Yeah well it's not like I can move out is it, not until I'm on full-time hours.

TARA Yeah I didn't mean, I just meant mums innit.

—

TARA You should tell them to shove that job.

STEPH I like that job.

TARA Yeah they've kept you hanging around ages though haven't they on that contract, like you're really good Steph you shouldn't have to be waiting to see whether they can be arsed to give you any hours.

STEPH Yeah well they said they're gunna put me on a training programme, so I can end up a manager.

TARA Oh right, great, well that's really great then.

STEPH Yeah after the summer they said.

TARA Oh right well I didn't know congratulations.

STEPH Thanks.

TARA Didn't they say something similiar to that last year though?

STEPH Well this time I'm right at the top of the list.

TARA Right well that's great then.

STEPH Yeah.

—

TARA They've really gone to town on the decorations in here haven't they?

STEPH What do you mean?

TARA All this shit. Looks like Brexit's been sick.

STEPH Yeah well they're doing a thing for the results tonight aren't they.

TARA Oh right, yeah course. I reckon it's just gunna fizzle don't you?

STEPH Not really.

TARA Like all the polls have said it's gunna be fine haven't they. I mean surely not enough people can be that stupid. Like I know some of our street probably did din't they, there's England flags everywhere but like no one I know at Uni even thinks it's a possibility/

STEPH Mum voted to leave.

TARA Oh. Oh right.

STEPH She put the flags up.

TARA Oh right yeah well it's not that they don't look, and I know my dad was a bit unsure, like older generation isn't it but/ I think

STEPH And I did.

TARA What?

STEPH I did.

TARA You?

STEPH Yeah.

TARA Oh right. I didn't, you never, I mean you didn't say anything/

STEPH Yeah well you hadn't been home have you.

TARA I have a bit Steph.

STEPH Yeah well not to see me.

TARA That's not fair.

STEPH Isn't it?

TARA What's that meant to mean?

STEPH It's meant to mean, like why have you even come out tonight? All you've done is sneer and talk about how gutted you are you've had to come back since Uni finished/

TARA Thats not, I haven't, I just want a job that's all, I'm just saying/

STEPH Coming back judging like, my life's not little Tara. It's not shit. Actually I'm happy, I'm really, really happy alright.

TARA I'm not judging anything actually/

STEPH *"It's not changed in here at all has it."*

TARA Well it hasn't!

STEPH Yeah why should it?

TARA I don't have a problem with your life Steph, and you can back off a bit alright 'cos this is my city too innit. I'm just saying I don't get it, like people do get the EU gives us money right?

STEPH Alright yeah I bet that's 'cos everyone at Uni thinks we're stupid don't they, like we don't know, like we don't know that. Yeah we do get some money maybe but actually that's not the point is it?

TARA What is the point then? Cos I'm literally not trying to be a dick but I don't get it Steph I don't.

STEPH The point is, the point is finally someone's asked us about what is going on and we're going to say something alright. I'm sick of people acting like we're stupid 'cos all we're allowed to care about is money alright just 'cos we don't have it. Some things are more important. Us having control over what we do, here in this country right is more important. Finally we're going to have some control here about what's going on /

TARA You do know you actually elect people to Europe don't you, you do know that it's/ not

STEPH Yes I fucking know. The point is people taking notice, right. Here. Like my mum says when was the last time some asked yeah? We've been sleeping in my aunty's spare room since Dad died /

TARA I know that Steph, I live round the corner it's not like /

STEPH And this is about saying time's something changed. We used to have options, like we used to, when there was fishing /

TARA Fishing? Your dad wasn't a fisherman Steph.

STEPH I fucking know that, that's not what I'm saying.

TARA Do you not think it's about time we stopped going on about fishing, like there's only so many fish anyway int there Steph, like do you not think we can all get a bit stuck.

STEPH That's not the point is it. The point is no one asked us did they, if they could just take it all away time and time again and then wonder why we're angry OK.

TARA I thought you were happy? You can't have it both ways can you, either this is the best place in the world or your life is crap and everything's gotta change, it can't be both can it? I mean you could do stuff you know. If you want to change things. You could make stuff happen.

84

STEPH Yeah and I am. Right here. Changing stuff.

TARA What stuff? Like what is this doing really Steph? Like Europe int /

STEPH I don't give a shit about Europe. Or Westminster or any of them. I don't trust any of them. Any of it. If you asked me did I wanna leave the House of Commons Tara I probably would have voted yes, I'd get rid of all of them 'cos I don't think they give a shit about us.

TARA What and you think that lot do? You think that lot in their helicopters and offshore finance and fucking pretend buffoonish, 'ordinary man' act do?

STEPH Yeah well at least they're pretending, right, noticed we exist. The rest is just, it's just wigs innit and weird rules and people grabbing expenses and Somebody-McFucking-Somebody staring my dad down at the Job Centre and saying he was being fined for not answering his phone one time, and Mrs. McShittyby who interviews me every time I apply for that fucking promotion and does this thing where she asks me why customer service is important to me, and haven't I had a warning, and what is it about this job that makes my soul ache when we all know I just want that extra quid an hour alright and I actually deserve it.

So yeah, let's get rid of it. Alright. Let's burn it all down and maybe this time when we've got control we can build something where we matter alright.

Pause.

TARA Yeah well that's the difference innit, you think you you're gunna matter more if we change things, if we blow it all up, and I look at how you're doing it and I know I'm gunna matter less /

STEPH What do / you

TARA I mean do you ever look at the people who are using this to, the people who are on your side Steph. Do you ever look at what they're saying, what they're making people feel they can–

Like, like I go in town today right to get your present and two grown men start shouting at me in the street /

STEPH Shouting what?

TARA What do you think Steph? Use your brain what do you think.

STEPH Well it's not like that normally / happens

TARA Yeah. It does actually. Here, in my home, my city, here more than it did at Uni which breaks my heart but yeah it does and it always has and it's been happening more now since all this fucking shit.

STEPH Well, that's, I've never noticed /

TARA Well you can afford not to notice.

Pause.

STEPH Well that's shit, fine that's shit Tara but I don't think that's got anything to do with what I just said. Does it? Like me and my mum aren't–

All I'm saying is we wanna be asked, we want some control over here to change stuff, over our lives here and suddenly we're racist.

TARA I'm not saying that am I.

STEPH Yeah well neither am I.

TARA All I'm saying is innit time we started to get on with something positive about what we are, I'm not sure shutting people out, blaming people, the wrong people/

STEPH Like you're blaming me right now.

TARA I'm not, Steph I'm really not I'm–

Pause.

Look I don't want to fall out alright, fucking hell I don't want to fall out on your birthday. Can we just not do this now.

STEPH I don't know.

Pause.

TARA Right. Right well I think I better go then.

STEPH OK. OK. Yeah maybe you had.

SCENE FOUR

Suddenly everything stops and a spotlight appears on our MC.

SONG – The Choice We've Made

MC
In the blink of an eye
Everything's different.
In the blink of an eye
Everything becomes apparent.
And in the blink of an eye
A change has come
And the volcano

(She clicks.)

Erupts

Whooping, cheering, the room explodes. SHEILA appears and hugs STEPH swinging her round. The MAN appears, celebrating with them. They revel in it.

ALL Yesssssssss.

SHEILA We've done it love. We've done it.

87

MAN Too bloody right we have. 52 to 48 they're saying.

Behind them ANNA comes up to the mic with MICHAL.

A huge cheer from the rest of the pub. NIGEL's on.

SHEILA This will show them right? This will really show them Steph. Where's Tara?

STEPH She had to go.

SHEILA Already, lightweight!

The MAN sprays prosecco all round the room. They all cheer again.

MAN WE ARE THE CHAMPIONS. Here, fill your boots. Here you go darling. And you. Tonight's the night. Tonight's the fucking night.

STEPH Someone's feeling flash.

MAN What's that darling?

STEPH I've not seen you in here before?

MAN Here for work, a mate took us out. See the town.

STEPH Oh right.

MAN Fuck knows how I'm going to get home now though, they've just buggered off.

STEPH Where you staying?

MAN Kirkella.

STEPH That's not even in Hull.

MAN Thought it looked too nice.

STEPH Oi.

MAN Maybe you could take me home eh? Show us a good time.

STEPH No thanks. You look a bit like my dad.

MAN Steady on.

STEPH If my dad wore suits.

MAN Alright mouth.

STEPH I'll have another drink though.

MAN Don't push your luck darling. Oii Oiiii we're about to hear more, look.

MC *(Spoken, getting everyone's attention.)* Nigel's on!

SONG – Nigel's on Nigel Farage

MC
Dare to dream
The dawn is breaking on an independent United Kingdom
This,
if the predictions now are right,
Will be a victory for real people
A victory for ordinary people
A victory for decent people
We have fought against the multinationals
We have fought against the big merchant banks
We have fought against big politics
We have fought against lies, corruption and deceit
And today; honesty, decency and belief in nation
I think
Now is going to win
And we will have done it without having to fight
Without a single bullet being fired
Without a single bullet being fired
Without a single bullet being fired
We'd have done it by damned hard work on the ground

Our MC takes off her Farage costume and applauds too much and for too long. The MAN joins her.

ANNA starts to sing (song 'Arahja') over the applause. She is defiant. MICHAL tries to pull her off the mic but she makes him join in.

MAN Too bloody right we have. Independent kingdom. Right ladies? Independent bloody kingdom.

He begins to sing 'Rule Britannia', a little incoherently. STEPH and SHEILA join in with the chorus.

RULE BRITANNIA BRITANNIA RULES THE WAVES

BRITONS NEVER NEVER NEVER SHALL BE SLAVES

For a bit it feels genuinely celebratory but it clashes with ANNA and MICHAL's song and the harder they try the more incoherent it gets, they don't really know the words, they can't keep going.

MAN Hey love, hey we're singing here. Alright. What is that shit? What is that shit anyway.

STEPH Don't/ it's alright

MAN No decent people are singing here, alright. Tonight we're celebrating aren't we? Hey can you hear? Can you? We're trying to sing here, actually have a moment aren't we.

STEPH I think she's just/singing

MAN No darling, it's alright I'll sort this. Look we're singing here OK.

RULE BRITTANIA BRITTANIA RULES THE WAVES

BRITAINS NEVER NEVER NEVER SHALL BE SLAVES

Hello? Are you going to/

STEPH Mum, I think maybe we / should

MAN No, Sheila was it? I'm right aren't I Sheila? What is that, what is that anyway? I can't understand it, can you? Fucking nonsense. Hello, alright can you hear me 'cos we're/ just

MC And suddenly there's no way back.

Because in that moment he grabs her. Anna. He catches her arms and this is what changes things forever. This is what–

Because he pulls her, he pulls her round and all they can hear suddenly is –

SONG – This Is England

MAN *(Sung.) This is England love. We speak fucking English here. Go home.*

STEPH Go home.

ANNA Go–

STEPH This is England love.

ANNA English–

STEPH Go–

Home–

Go–

(The words 'go home' build and echo around the space, becoming a chorus.)

ANNA This is–

MAN *(Sung.)* And I spit.

ANNA
Into my face he spits.
This cartoon carved from colonial crust.
He spits out the venom he's been trained to curate
He spits out generations and generations of inherited hate
He spits out the rhetoric he's heard and Nigel's words and clichés slurred.

MAN

My saliva is both metaphor and simile for a feeling that's always
lived in me
Bred in the petri dish of our national identity
I spit my spit into the face of another human because in that second
In the blink of an eye
I've got allies.
Because for me it's not about Leave or Remain,
It's about permission given to my deep-down distain.
It's about taking back control
Because England is mine, England is mine, England is mine,
England is mine.
And it owes *me* a living.

ANNA Go. Home.

STEPH Go. Home.

ANNA This is England love.

STEPH We speak English here.

ANNA This is England. This is England. This is–

STEPH Go home.

ANNA

As he spits, this man, this caveman, I force myself to repress
Because back to *his* view of this world I refuse to regress.
I push him into some distant part of my brain
And find myself drawn to *her,* standing there choosing to abstain
Steph.
Because Steph watches.
She watches but she doesn't stop it.
She doesn't stop it.
She does not stop it.
And this is the moment in history that we lose our voice.
The moment in history defined by a choice.

Where in five years, ten years, twenty years
The repercussions of this will still have us drying our tears.
This isn't about the box she ticked or the side she picked
It's about how as humans we choose to live
About the communities we choose to build
Because they'll divide us all eventually don't you worry about that.
Because of how we look or who we love or how much we earn
or where we're from.
If all we have is each other then where are you right now?
Because I need you.
I really fucking need you right now because I can't do this on
my own.

(The song breaks.)

Because this is the chance to make a difference.
This is the chance to fight for people like me.
Because we are here and we deserve better.
Because we will not wait forever.
Because one day you might look up and we will be gone, and be
sure that's what you want, really be sure that's what you want.
Because there will be no turning back.
Because that loss will not be mine. It will be yours. And it will
be momentous.
This is your chance.

Steph?

Wait.

'Go Home' begins to echo round the space again.

STEPH doesn't move.

STEPH But I don't move.

ANNA She doesn't help.

STEPH And in our eyes/

93

ANNA In our hearts / *W naszych sercach*

STEPH Something is broken then.

ANNA Something is really broken then.

SCENE FIVE

ANNA and STEPH outside. It is very still.

STEPH Hey.

ANNA Hello.

—

STEPH Are you ok?

ANNA What?

STEPH Sorry I saw, in there I/

ANNA I know.

STEPH Right. Right. I just wanted to check if you were OK.

—

I'm, I would've said something /

ANNA OK.

STEPH In there I would've /

ANNA Right. You didn't though /

STEPH He seemed alright you see, before, and like I'm sure he didn't mean /

ANNA Steph /

STEPH It was just bad timing, the song, at that moment if you hadn't have /

ANNA If I hadn't?

STEPH If you had just been a little less, I dunno visible / then

ANNA Right /

STEPH I just mean /

ANNA A little less. If I had just been a little less.

—

STEPH People think that, they think that things are simple, that you can just decide in a moment, but like not everything is just good or bad is it? Sometimes things happen and you don't mean them to but if you really believe in something, if you–

—

I don't know what to do now.

ANNA You could go?

STEPH I can't.

ANNA What?

STEPH I don't know why but I can't.

ANNA OK.

—

You take some responsibility. You could say you were sorry. You could say you were sorry and you never thought this would happen, and you see now your mistake and you didn't mean for this to be about us, and you've changed your mind because this is just, because this is–

Because you didn't understand and what have you done? What have you done really?

STEPH Right.

ANNA Right.

STEPH And then?

ANNA And then, and then I don't know Steph because you're just this girl I snogged once in a shitty bar and I don't know you, I don't know you at all.

—

STEPH I can't because I'm not.

ANNA What?

STEPH Sorry. Say I'm sorry.

ANNA Right.

STEPH I mean I am sorry, with the man there, and not saying anything, with you, I am sorry but tonight, we have worked really hard tonight and I have been waiting for this chance a long time and I'm not sorry it happened.

ANNA Right.

STEPH I am really sorry he did that to you. I am. But this is, tonight is, this is going to be a good thing you'll see.

—

Anna?

—

STEPH turns to go. ANNA doesn't want to but something makes her call her back.

ANNA Steph /

STEPH Yes?

ANNA Could you /

STEPH Yes?

ANNA Could you stay just for a minute /

STEPH Yes if you / want me

ANNA Michal has, he's getting my coat /

STEPH OK /

ANNA And just for a minute I don't want to /

She sits down. They sit together not facing one another.

ANNA Thank you.

STEPH It's OK.

ANNA We don't have to talk.

STEPH OK.

ANNA I think if we don't talk maybe it will be alright.

They sit still for a long time.

STEPH Anna /

ANNA Yes?

STEPH Are you frightened?

ANNA Yes. All the time.

STEPH Me too.

—

Do you think it will ever stop?

ANNA It has to sometime doesn't it? Sometime it has to end.

The End.

EPILOGUE

Now it is just the MC speaking to the audience, soul-to-soul.

MC There is a story we tell ourselves about what we were and what we need to once again become. Isn't there? About how we were safe, and mighty, independent and sovereign and free. About how we won wars and conquered cities and had pride in something bigger than ourselves.

About how that made things bearable.

And we need it right? We need it even if it's a myth because it is something large and we can cling to it.

But it's not true. And more importantly it's led us somewhere dark and fractured and alone.

So tonight I want to say there is a different story and we can make it. All of us here tonight. All of us in this city.

There is a story where 'them' becomes 'us', where it is not our difference or our past but the future that we build together that defines us.

Tonight I want to say we can decide what happens next.
Us. Here.

Leave or Remain, British or European, Hull or Leeds, or even down south if we must, whatever, I don't care 'cos what really matters is what we do next. Together.

Together we can build a story that isn't obscured by fear or loss.

We can do that. I know we can.

If we just open those big fucking hearts I know this city's got, I know each one of you here tonight has got.

Because I've seen us time and time again build a city from ashes on the ground. I've seen us.

If there's one thing I believe in it's that.

If there's one thing I know to be true it's that.

Because we can catch each other right? If we try we can. And we will right?

At least I hope we will.

Tonight.

I fucking hope we will.

ANNA I fucking hope we will.
Mam nadzieję.

Gradually the others join in with her, ANNA leads the chant in Polish, the MC in English. It builds.

I hope we will. I hope we will. I hope we will. I hope we will. I hope we will. I hope we will. I hope we will.
Mam nadzieję.

Stop.

I

Fucking Hope.

MC
I stand here before you tonight to look you in the eye and ask;
(Sung.)

What *really* happens?

When a desolate island defined by what it was decides to
delegate to its descendants the chance to redesign its destiny?
What *really* happens?

When a sickly city mocked, shamed, forgotten, deprived and
disposed is given the chance to prove it's been misdiagnosed?
What *really* happens?

When the people so regularly suffocated, raised on severity,
shackled by austerity come up for air, poke their heads out
to see what's still there?
And it's here in this bar by the interchange
That the whole entire world did change.